The Confident
Performer

*This book is dedicated to my mother who remains for me an inspiration
and a model of professional caring, even after her death.*

The Confident Performer

DAVID ROLAND

Heinemann
A division of Reed Elsevier Inc.
361 Hanover Street
Portsmouth, NH 03801-3912
http://www.heinemann.com

Offices and agents throughout the world

First published in 1997 by
Currency Press Ltd, Sydney, Australia and
Nick Hern Books Ltd, London, UK
This edition published in 1998

Library of Congress Cataloging-in-Publication Data
On file at the Library of Congress

ISBN 0 – 325 – 00092 – 1

Cover designed by Anaconda Graphics / Trevor Hood
Line drawings at the beginning of each chapter by Kelvin Robertson
Typeset by Currency Press in 11pt Nebraska
Printed by Southwood Press, Marrickville NSW Australia

Contents

Acknowledgments

My deepest gratitude goes to the students and staff of the Wollongong Conservatorium of Music at the University of Wollongong, and the Canberra School of Music at the Institute of the Arts, Australian National University. Thank you for allowing me to research and try out my new ideas in the early days of my investigation into performance anxiety.

Thank you to the numerous individual artists and performance groups who have requested my services and in the process, have provided me with the continuing insights into the application of mental skills to performing. Thank you to the artists who have specifically allowed me to use their case histories to illustrate certain points throughout the book.

Thank you to those performance teachers, artists and colleagues who have provided direct comments and feedback on the manuscript and on my work as it has progressed: Peggy Croskey, Virginia Gallagher, Gordon Beattie, Coral Haddock, Jean Callaghan, Lydia Illeva, Gary McPherson, Jeff Bond and Michael Williamson.

Most of the creative writing period was spent with Peter, Julie, and Tom the cat from Swanhaven — thankyou for the use of your holiday cabins. Thanks to the Varuna Writers Centre and Chas and Sandra Tarbey who provided me with the space and environment to produce the final drafts.

Thank you to my professional colleagues, Saroja Srinivasan and David Goldman, who have been a support simply by being there.

Thank you to Steven Samios for the diagram illustrations throughout the book. Thank you to my wife, Leah Roland for her loving support and contributions during the publication process, especially when things became very hectic.

Introduction

When I was a child, the first significant experience with music I remember was listening to the small record collection owned by my parents. I became particularly fascinated with an album of music called *Tijuana Brass* — a collection of Spanish bull fighting tunes played on brass instruments. I and my three siblings made toy trumpets from plastic building sets and performed for our parents, pretending to play to the strains of the Tijuana Brass. The music was bright, rhythmic and exciting. I was equally excited by the attention I gained from my parents and my pleasure in being able to make them laugh at our antics.

Many performers remember distinct moments in their childhood when they first became aware of how music, dance or acting made a deep impression on them. A professional rock singer told me that, from an early age, he would mime pop tunes on the radio. When he was a young teenager, he joined a rock band with school friends. He had a troubled life, both at home and at school, and making music was the only activity that seemed to go right for him. He and his band went on to achieve international success and today he believes that music 'saved' him from a potentially less fortunate life.

I recently heard a prominent cellist being interviewed on the radio, describing how she was encouraged to learn the piano as a child by her music-loving parents. Although she felt some affection for the piano, she felt no passion. Her parents, being amateur musicians, occasionally invited other musicians to their home to play chamber music. During one of these recitals she heard the cello being played. She felt inexplicably drawn to its sound and asked her parents to let her drop the piano lessons and take up the cello instead — an instrument she has felt an intense passion for ever since. Episodes such as this suggest there is a psychology to performance which starts from the very first time we are attracted to it, and this underlying attraction stays with us when we perform as adults.

Over the last six years my professional work has been increasingly oriented towards helping performers extend themselves through psychological applications in performance. As part of my postgraduate studies in psychology, I conducted some fascinating research which led me to a greater understanding of the problem of performance anxiety and how to manage it. One study required me to interview many celebrated local and international musicians and singers to discover how they managed performance anxiety and how they approached performance at a psychological level. This enabled me to gain insight into the psychology of performance, and in recent years I have extended the initial work on performance anxiety to cover many other aspects of performance enhancement, both with musicians and singers, and more recently with dancers and actors.

This book introduces all practising performers, both amateur and professional, to ideas on the mental aspects of performance, which can lead to tremendous improvements in performing. As well it discusses physiological and behavioural aspects of performing. Artists will be able to gain greater consistency in their performances and increased confidence in performing. If you are having some difficulties in your performing which you haven't been able to overcome through technical means, then the mental approaches covered in this book could well provide the answers for you.

Many performers are initially doubtful about the usefulness of adopting a mental approach to performing. This is understandable, because it is a relatively new area, yet I am convinced it is a crucial one. I often tell performers that, when preparing for a performance, they are not only preparing the external aspects of performance, that is, music, dance, drama, but they are also preparing the internal means of producing it — themselves. If they leave out this second, crucial element, then they will not succeed.

After reading this book, you may change some of the ways you prepare for a performance. Be assured that all the ideas and techniques presented here have been tried by hundreds of performers and have helped many of them.

Many of the skills discussed in this book are equally applicable to any kind of 'performer', not just those in the conventional performing arts. For example, if you are involved in public speaking, giving demonstrations, selling, taking examinations, or going for job interviews, you will find these ideas very helpful.

An audio tape has been produced to accompany the book. Its purpose is to guide you through some of the more practical aspects of the book, such as relaxation exercises, to enhance the effectiveness these techniques have for you.

1 Performance Anxiety

We are so largely the playthings of ... our fears. To one, fear
of the dark, to another, of physical pain, to a third, of public
ridicule, to a fourth of poverty, to a fifth of loneliness — for
all of us our particular creature lurks in ambush.
Hugh Walpole

THE GAME OF ANXIETY

Do you ever experience tension, ' butterflies in the stomach' or nervous
anticipation? You might be relieved to know that all artists experience some anxiety
about performance. Artists who experience anxiety to a severe extent call this
'stage fright'. Whatever word you use, some self-doubt about your ability to perform
is perfectly normal and understandable. In fact, most experienced performers
become concerned if they don't experience some nervous anticipation before
performing. Let's have a look at what I'll call here 'performance anxiety' to
understand what it is, why it comes about and what to do about it if it is getting the
better of you.

> You never stop being nervous. The first concert in San Francisco was the scariest
> night of my life ... going out to face 22,000 people ... it was like jumping off the top
> of a building, without a parachute, hoping that you landed on a haystack. I hadn't
> eaten for two nights; I hadn't slept for a night and a half. At the last moment, I
> realised that I had been rehearsing this for six weeks, that I'd played the Phantom
> for three and a half years, I must know the words by now.
> *Actor Michael Crawford speaking about his role in the production of Phantom of the Opera
> in San Francisco,* Sydney Morning Herald, *5 May 1992.*

> I am not fitted to give concerts. The audience intimidates me, I feel choked by its
> breath, paralysed by its curious glances, struck dumb by all those strange faces.
> *Frederic Chopin in Kimball, Petersen & Johnson, 1990.*

> A little boy in his school uniform climbs on stage. This time it's verse speaking for seven
> years and under. For a few anxious moments he's so overcome by stage fright he can't
> remember his lines. He looks in anguish towards his mother before he suddenly
> remembers his words. He recites in a voice so quiet it's impossible to hear him.
> *From an article on performance competitions for children,* Australian, *20 August 1994.*

WHAT IS PERFORMANCE ANXIETY?

As the term 'stage fright' suggests, artists feel apprehensive about approaching the stage and performing, even though they are doing what they love. Typically, anxious artists experience a variety of bodily and mental symptoms.

The bodily symptoms can include:
- muscle tension
- shaking of various parts of the body
- increased heart rate
- sweating
- hot or cold flushes
- nausea
- dry mouth
- 'butterflies in the stomach'
- desire to go frequently to the toilet
- an adrenalin rush

The mental symptoms can include:
- negative thoughts
- distraction
- a feeling of impending doom
- memory blanks
- a feeling of panic

You may have noticed that the amount of anxiety you experience before performing varies for different situations. Some of the common situations in which artists experience more anxiety are:

> Marjorie was a serious amateur piano player who noticed a distinct difference in her levels of anxiety depending upon the situations she was performing in. She was able to perform comfortably for her music teacher, family and friends but experienced anxiety when performing in public, despite being a talented pianist. Her worst performance experience occurred when she was the main artist at a major concert given by her school of music. She became so nervous that she found the notes were 'dancing about' on her music score and the sweat from her hands was so profuse that she needed to wipe down the piano keys with a cloth between movements!
>
> Severe anxiety can be a problem because it reduces artists' spontaneity and feeling of security during the performance and can lead to mistakes being made. After a performance where artists believe they have not performed well, they are left feeling let down and perhaps embarrassed, thinking that they appeared badly in the eyes of the audience and fellow artists. Having a bad experience in one performance can lead to artists feeling less confident about their next performances.

- when performing a solo
- in examinations or competitions
- in auditions
- on opening night
- where the performance is for an especially important occasion
- where there is a person in the audience that is held in high esteem by the artists

In contrast, artists experience less anxiety when they are playing for an audience who they don't feel is particularly demanding of them, when they are performing something they have performed many times before, or when they feel they have really mastered their material.

THE POSITIVE EXPERIENCE OF ANXIETY

You might be pleased to know that there is a positive side to anxiety. The fact is that anxiety is a *normal* emotion and everyone experiences anxiety in everyday situations. Situations where people, other than performing artists, experience anxiety include public speaking, sports competitions, examinations, job interviews and parties. As a performing artist, you would be less than human if you did not experience some anxiety in performing because you are being assessed by other people — an audience.

Every professional artist I have ever spoken to confesses to experiencing some anxiety before performing, even when they have had many years of performance experience. They also said their anxiety was positive when they were able to manage it and use it to energise their performance. Instead of thinking of it as anxiety, they thought of it more as excitement, or an eagerness to go on stage and perform. When they viewed it this way, they found their anxiety could lift their performance to a level over and above what they had been able to achieve in practice or rehearsals. This suggests that a feeling of 'nervous excitement' is a necessary part of performing.

If you're not nervous you're dead.

Saxophone player

The idea that some anxiety can be beneficial to a performance sounds strange to a lot of performers, particularly those in their early years of performing. Younger artists usually concentrate more on the technical aspects of their performance and so are more concerned about getting it right. Accomplished artists are more focussed on bringing their performance to life because they can rely more on their technique being in place.

I feel that the only way I can really make a good performance of anything is to go with the flow in the music and forget about the technique. Once I'm in there I should be making music and not playing notes.

Trombone player

A little anxiety before performing helps you become alert and focussed on what you have to do. It can be an occupational hazard for artists who are giving the same performance night after night to become too blase about their performances, and leave the freshness out of it. Ultimately, the joy of performing is to bring to life a piece of theatre, music or dance in a way that is inspiring for you and the audience.

> I've found very often if I've gone up on stage and I'm not nervous I don't give my best performance. In fact it's probably the most correct performance but it's missing something.
>
> *Pianist*

OPTIMUM ANXIETY

Research in psychology supports the idea that some anxiety is helpful for the performing artist. A little anxiety increases a person's ability to perform simple tasks better and more quickly, up to an optimum point. If the anxiety goes beyond this optimum point, then the person's performance becomes worse.

The diagram below shows that when you are totally relaxed, you are likely to perform well. As your anxiety increases, you will reach a certain level at which you perform at your best for that particular performance. If your anxiety goes beyond this, you will find you become overwhelmed by your anxiety, and will start to make mistakes, and you may even eventually lose it altogether if your anxiety gets too high. Every artist's optimum level of anxiety will be different. Research has found

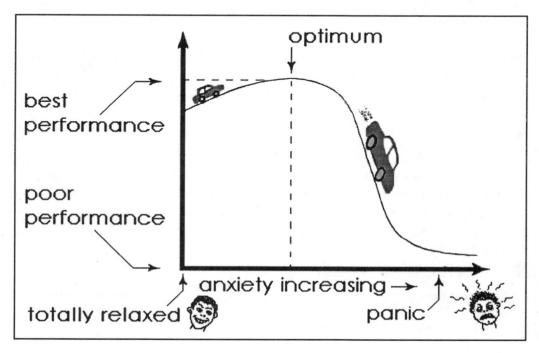

that experienced and less experienced artists reach their peak of anxiety at different times. Experienced artists let their anxiety peak just before performing, and once they begin performing, their anxiety level falls. Inexperienced artists reach the peak of their anxiety during their performance. This is why anxiety in the inexperienced artist can have a more disastrous effect on performance than it does in the case of the experienced artist.

> To play sober, to play straight, is like going to the dentist, I suppose. You're very, very nervous until the actual thing is taking place, then you call on some reserve inside you which is just waiting. Once you've got past the first couple of songs you've broken the ice for yourself and for everyone else. I always relax after I've played my first solo.
> *Eric Clapton, rock singer and guitarist, from Kohut & Kohut 1994*

> Offstage I'm not too sure of myself, but onstage I'm in command.
> *Liberace in Fowles, 1992*

STAGES OF ANXIETY

During your performance career, you will go through different phases of experiencing performance anxiety. In my own research, I found that professional artists often experienced intense anxiety in particular stages of their careers, such as when they were training, or when they first took on professional engagements or a new performance challenge, such as becoming a principal of an orchestra or taking on a lead role. If you are a younger artist, keep in mind that your anxiety will generally decrease as you gain more performance experience.

> Steve, the drummer from the up-and-coming rock group, Tumbleweed, told me that his group's first gig in an overseas country made him very nervous beforehand, he said, ' We knew that it had to be a good show because we were starting out from scratch in a new country. We went out there, it went well and we had fun.
> Rolling Stone *magazine, 1993*

The majority of artists experience anxiety only on stage and not in their life generally, so their anxiety is specific to performing. However, some artists also experience significant anxiety outside of their performing life. One reason for this can be that the artists are going through a period of low self-esteem or are feeling generally inadequate. If the artists are nervous or tense people most of the time, then they might be experiencing generalised anxiety. In either of these cases, it would be helpful to address these broader causes of anxiety by consulting with a mental health professional, such as a psychologist.

THE FIGHT OR FLIGHT RESPONSE AND THREAT

All humans have an in-built physiological response called the fight or flight response, which helps us when we are under threat. In prehistoric times, this would have been a life threatening event such as an attack from a wild animal or from a neighbouring tribe. When we feel threatened, the body becomes mobilised for action, either to escape from the threat or to fight back. The decision about which to do depends on the person's assessment of which will produce the best outcome.

In the fight or flight response, there is a chain of events which takes place extremely quickly when we feel threatened, whether that threat is real or imagined. Hormones, such as adrenalin and cortisone, are secreted quickly into the bloodstream, sending messages around the body to instigate various changes for action.

These changes involve the heart pumping harder and faster, with blood flow to the legs, arms, shoulders and back being increased. At the same time, the flow of blood to parts of the body that are not essential for action — the digestive system, skin, face, genitals and kidneys — is reduced. More oxygen is taken in with faster breathing, the pupils of the eyes enlarge, saliva production stops and sweating starts.

The fight or flight response can produce the following symptoms:

- muscles tense
- heart beats faster and harder
- breathing becomes faster
- sweating occurs
- coldness in the hands and feet
- skin becomes paler
- mouth becomes drier

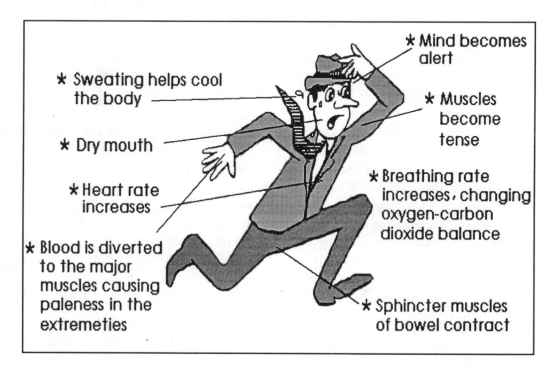

- butterflies in the stomach and/or nausea
- desire to go to the toilet
- mental alertness or loss of concentration
- panic
- becoming light headed
- hypersensitive to sounds, sights, smells

THE FIGHT OR FLIGHT RESPONSE AND PERFORMING

In a performance, the threat is not a direct physical threat such as a sabre-toothed tiger but a more subtle psychological threat, which can be perceived differently from artist to artist. These threats largely centre around artists feeling they are being evaluated. Because a performance is very short in duration, compared with the enormous amount of time and effort that is put into its preparation, performing has a 'do or die' quality. Artists know that their expertise is being assessed on what they produce in a few minutes and not on the work they have done over the days, months or years.

When artists are feeling threatened by a performance, they will mentally create one or more of these 'threats':

- overestimate their chance of failing in the performance
- overestimate the difficulty of the performance
- overestimate the consequences of potential failure
- underestimate their ability to cope with the demands of the performance

Artists may feel threatened because they believe they are inadequately prepared, not good enough technically, the audience is unfriendly in some way and will not respond well or they will lose their reputation completely if they don't produce a stunning performance. They may also perceive high expectations from teachers, parents and fellow performers.

In our civilised society, it is not likely that the audience will harm artists physically if the performance is not up to scratch. At the extreme, it may boo or yell abusive remarks, or walk out. Anxious performers often forget that the audience is there to support them — it wants the performance to go well.

> The public comes to the theatre not because they want to heckle and see things go wrong. They come because they hope it's going to be wonderful, and they're going to join in that one special occasion, that special night.
>
> *Ingrid Bergman in Sinden 1987*

The perceived threat to artists is a psychological one but the body still responds as if it is being physically threatened. This is because the primitive subconscious part of the brain which initiates the fight or flight response doesn't distinguish between a psychological and a physical threat. The fight or flight response is designed for actions such as running, fighting or climbing up a tree — rather inappropriate actions for most artists!

Before a performance, you have probably experienced the sensations of wanting to get away (flight) or feeling desperate to get it over with (fight). Most performances require fine motor control and sophisticated mind/body coordination. For this reason, it is not a good idea to let the fight or flight response build up too much, although, as explained earlier, a little controlled anxiety is helpful. The next chapter explains how to minimise the build-up of the fight or flight response.

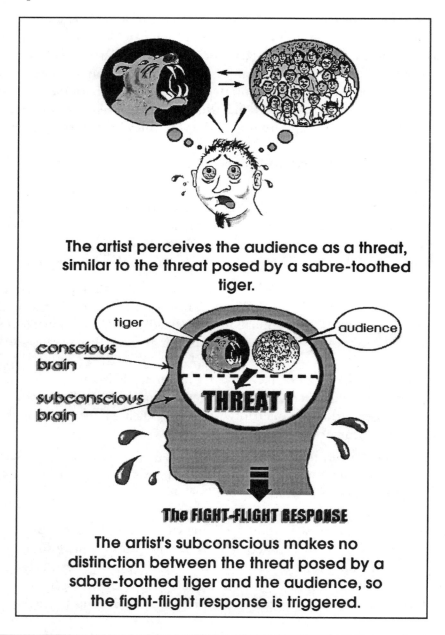

The artist perceives the audience as a threat, similar to the threat posed by a sabre-toothed tiger.

tiger

audience

conscious brain

subconscious brain

THREAT!

The FIGHT-FLIGHT RESPONSE

The artist's subconscious makes no distinction between the threat posed by a sabre-toothed tiger and the audience, so the fight-flight response is triggered.

A Concept for Understanding Anxiety

A human emotion such as anxiety can be broken down into three responses: mental, behavioural and physiological. Mental responses are those that involve the thinking processes and are not observable by anyone except by the artist. Behavioural responses are those that involve actions which are observable by others. Physiological responses involve the physical changes brought about by the fight or flight response.

Examples of mental response:
- loss of concentration
- distraction
- thoughts about failure.

Examples of behavioural response:
- tension
- agitation
- acting in a panicky way.

Examples of physiological response:
- increased heart rate
- nausea
- hormone secretion
- increased breathing rate

The mental, behavioural and physiological responses combine to give us the feeling we call anxiety, nervousness or stage fright. When you have become anxious in the past, you might not have been conscious of how you responded in each of the three systems, but you would have experienced a reaction in each of these systems. The overall effect of anxiety is that it makes you feel as though you are losing self-control.

A particular feature of anxiety is that it 'feeds off itself' and becomes stronger even though the 'threat' hasn't changed. Just think about your own experience of anxiety for a moment. As you approached a performance in which you started to become nervous, you might remember that you became aware of physical sensations, such as an adrenalin rush or a churning stomach. Following this, you might have thought (subconsciously) something like 'I'm starting to feel nervous; I'm starting to have doubts about whether I can do it', and then you found your physiological response becoming stronger. As your physiological response became stronger, such as your heart rate increasing, you would have felt you were losing control over the situation. Because you felt your loss of control increasing, you would have felt the threat of performing growing, and this would have set off a further increase in your mental, behavioural and physiological responses. As a result of the feedback you get from your initial sensations of nervousness, the feeling of anxiety grows and the threat of the performance seems to grow bigger and bigger each minute.

You may have experienced a time when you had to perform at short notice. As a result, you had little time for a build-up of anxiety to occur and you went on to perform without becoming too anxious. On the occasions when you have had to wait a longer time to perform (for example in an exam, at an eisteddfod), you probably found that your anxiety increased the longer you had to wait for your performance.

The simple conclusion is not to let performance anxiety build up in the first place. When you feel the first signs of anxiety appearing, this is the signal that you

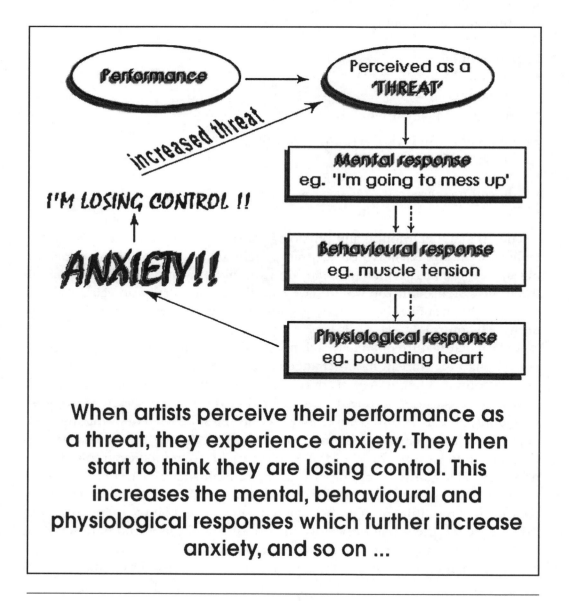

When artists perceive their performance as a threat, they experience anxiety. They then start to think they are losing control. This increases the mental, behavioural and physiological responses which further increase anxiety, and so on ...

need to nip anxiety in the bud by using methods described in the following chapters. You can use methods which act at each of the three levels, mental, behavioural and physiological.

ACTIVITY: YOUR ANXIETY RESPONSE

Begin to become aware of how you respond when you are feeling nervous or anxious at any time, not just when performing. How does it affect your thinking (mental response)? How does it affect your actions (behavioural response)? What physiological effects does it have? The more you begin to become conscious of these responses, the more you will be able to manage your anxiety and make it work for you.

2 Taking The Challenge: Thinking Your Way Through The Performance

We are what we think. All that we are arises with our
thoughts. With our thoughts, we make our world.
Buddha

PERCEIVING IT AS A CHALLENGE

If you see a performance as a threat, you will experience anxiety. However, you don't have to perceive it in this way — you can also view it is as a challenge. The concept of a challenge is totally different from that of a threat. When working with performing artists, I often ask the question 'What do you experience when you see something as a challenge, and what do you experience when you see something as a threat?'. Here is a summary of the frequent responses artists give me:

CHALLENGE

- I'm choosing to take it on.
- I feel determined.
- I'm prepared and willing to overcome obstacles.
- I'm prepared to take risks.
- I often feel a sense of excitement.
- I often set specific goals.
- I enjoy a sense of achievement when I've accomplished my goal.
- I mostly think positively about myself.
- I am generally optimistic that I can do it.
- I feel I am the one in control.

THREAT

- I want to avoid it.
- I feel like giving up.

- I find myself being stopped by obstacles.
- I try to play it safe.
- I often feel afraid.
- I don't plan what I'm going to do very well.
- I just feel a sense of relief when it's over.
- I mostly think negatively about myself.
- I tend to be pessimistic about my chances.
- I feel that circumstances around me are in control of me.

I began to discriminate between fear and excitement. The two, though very close, are completely different. Fear is negative excitement, choking your imagination. Real excitement produces an energy that overcomes apprehension and makes you want to close in on your goal.

Twyla Tharp, dancer in Tharp, 1992.

When you view something as a challenge, you are likely to be nervous at times.

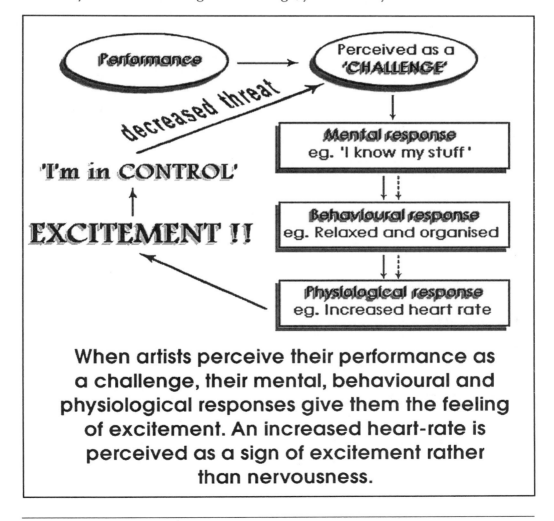

When artists perceive their performance as a challenge, their mental, behavioural and physiological responses give them the feeling of excitement. An increased heart-rate is perceived as a sign of excitement rather than nervousness.

But when you are operating in the challenge mode, you do not stay focussed on this; instead, you focus on what you are trying to achieve and you interpret your nervousness as a readiness or excitement to get on with the job.

If you look at the three systems concept of anxiety again, you will see that the perception of a performance as a challenge brings about responses different from perceiving it as a threat. On the mental level, the performers will be thinking of positive reasons why they will be able to perform well, and at a behavioural level, they will be relaxed and together. At a physiological level they will still experience an increase in the physiological response, but they will interpret this response as excitement rather than anxiety.

A few years ago, I conducted some research with anxious musicians to see if I could help them become more relaxed about performing. First, I asked them to give a performance during which I measured their heart rate and anxiety level. Then I ran some training sessions with them to help them gain control of their anxiety. After the sessions were completed they gave a second performance and I again measured their heart rate and anxiety level. They reported feeling much more comfortable during their second performance and felt they had played better. However, what was interesting was that their heart rate was just as high in the second performance as in the first. Because they had begun to see performing as a challenge rather than a threat, the increase in heart rate during the second performance was interpreted as a positive experience.

If you were told that you had just won a large amount of money in a competition, it is likely that your heart rate would go up, as it would if you had got a huge fright. This suggests it is how you perceive your physiological changes in performance that determines how you respond to them.

If you are performing because you love what you do and wish to be successful at it, then perceiving performing as a challenge makes a lot of sense. However, if you are performing because of pressure from others, then you will continue to experience performing as a threat. If this is the case, it would be wise to question whether performing is the right thing for you to be doing.

Changing Your Mental Response

To change your mental response in a performance from perceiving it as a threat to perceiving it as a challenge, it is necessary to look at the type of thinking referred to as self-talk. At every waking moment we 'talk' to ourselves about our experiences and things happening around us. We might think 'It's a nice day today' or 'I'm feeling fantastic today'. Likewise, as a performer, you are talking to yourself about your perception of you as a performer, such as 'I feel really prepared for this performance', 'I'm looking forward to my solo', 'I'm dreading this performance'.

The actor Laurence Olivier gives a good example of changing the perception of a performance from a threat into a challenge. He was asked for advice by the actor John Mills on how to deal with first-night nerves. Olivier told him:

> There's a trick I've used on occasions and I find it works. Try it. Go to the theatre early on the first night, and get made up well in advance of the curtain. Then walk on to the stage and imagine that the curtain is already up and that you are facing the audience. Look out at them and shout, ' You are about to see the greatest fucking performance of your entire theatre-going lives. And I will be giving it. You lucky people.' Tell them that once or twice. Then go back to your dressing room and relax, and you'll find that when the curtain does go up you'll have the necessary confidence.
>
> *Laurence Olivier, Spoto, 1992.*

Perceiving the performance as a threat is an example of negative self-talk and perceiving it as a challenge is an example of positive self-talk. You can boost your self-confidence through positive self-talk or undermine it through negative self-talk. Most artists aren't aware of whether their self-talk is positive or negative. The reason for this is that everyone develops habits in thinking, in the same way that they develop habits in other things. Most of our thinking is at a subconscious level so we're not normally conscious of it.

To illustrate how thinking can affect the outcome of a performance, let's analyse the following example:

A	B	C
Performance situation	Self-talk	Consequence
Heart beating quickly before performing	'My heart is going crazy, I'm losing control, I'm going to make a mess of this.'	Lose control and give a bad performance
Heart beating quickly before performing	'My heart is beating faster, that's normal, keep focussed on my breathing and I'll be fine.'	Maintain control and give a good performance

You will notice that the different self-talk in Column B brought about different consequences for the same performance situation. In the first instance, the artist acknowledged his physiological response in a panicky way and drew negative conclusions from this; that is the performance was perceived as a threat. In the second instance, the physiological response was realistically acknowledged and positive conclusions were drawn from it; that is the performance was perceived as a challenge.

If your self-talk can have such a dramatic influence over how you perform, then start taking notice of it (see Activity 1). Research has shown that simply thinking a negative thought, without acting on it, produces physiological changes in the body, so be particular about your thoughts, as they are powerful!

Sometimes people believe that thinking positive thoughts means forcing yourself to think something you don't really believe in. It is important that you develop positive self-talk which honestly acknowledges what is happening, so that it is believable when you think it. For example, if you really haven't rehearsed sufficiently for a performance, then you can't say to yourself 'This is going to be a fabulous performance because I know my work inside out', because you're not going to really believe this. You would be better off saying 'I don't know my work as well as I would like; however, I will do my best and learn from this performance what I need to work on for the next one.'

THE FOUR SUBPERSONALITIES OF ANXIETY

Edmund Bourne in his book, *The Anxiety and Phobia Workbook*, has identified four types of anxious thinking. These subpersonalities can be observed in anxious artists at a subconscious level and are called here 'the Worrier', 'the Critic', 'the Victim' and 'the Perfectionist'.

THE WORRIER

The Worrier promotes anxiety by anticipating the worst possible outcome, overestimating the chances of failure. The Worrier's favourite expression is 'What if ...?' The Worrier is the type of person who, when you suggest going on a Sunday picnic, starts anticipating bad weather days before the event. An example of Worrier-style thinking in performance is 'What if I have a memory blank in the performance?'

THE CRITIC

The Critic promotes low self-esteem by pointing out your perceived weaknesses and limitations and putting you down whenever it can. Some of the Critic's favourite expressions are 'You're kidding yourself, how could you be so stupid'. An example of Critic-style thinking in a performance is 'This audience is going to think you are a joke compared to the other performers. They'll want their money back!'

THE VICTIM

The Victim promotes depression and makes you feel helpless and powerless. The Victim is good at seeing obstacles to success — all the reasons why the circumstances are against you. The Victim's favourite expression is 'I can't'. An example of Victim-style thinking in a performance is 'I can't be a good dancer because I started too late', or 'my legs aren't the right shape'.

THE PERFECTIONIST

The Perfectionist promotes constant stress. It is always pushing you to do better, but you can never do quite well enough to satisfy the Perfectionist, despite how well others around you might say you are doing. The Perfectionist's favourite expressions are 'I must' and 'I should'. An example of Perfectionist-style thinking in a performance is 'I must get everything right otherwise the whole performance will be a failure'.

It is helpful to identify which of the four sub-personalities you tend to follow in your thinking so you can counteract them with positive self-talk. Once you become aware of how the mental habits you have formed affect your performance, then you can change them if they don't help you.

WRITING A LIST OF HELPFUL SELF-TALK

The way to counteract the negative sub-personalities and break old habits in thinking is to consciously practise the new ones. An excellent way of doing this is to write a list of positive self-talk for the four different stages of the performance process. These are:

PREPARATION: the period of time from the point you first know you will give a particular performance until the moment you arrive at the venue.

BEFORE: the period of time while at the performance venue before you go on stage to perform.

DURING: the period of time while you are performing.

AFTER: the period of time after you have finished your performance and while you are still evaluating it in your mind.

1. PREPARING FOR THE PERFORMANCE:

OBJECTIVES

- Focus on specific preparation tasks for the performance.
- Get into a positive mode of thinking from the start.
- Emphasise following a pre-performance routine.

EXAMPLES

- I'll work out a plan to prepare for this performance.
- What are the goals I want to achieve in this performance?
- I'm looking forward to this challenge.
- I will give it my best.
- If I have self-doubts, I can get help and practise my positive self-talk.
- I'll organise some preliminary performances to run through my piece, role etc.
- If I feel nervous sometimes, that's natural; it means this performance is important to me.

2. BEFORE THE PERFORMANCE:

OBJECTIVES

- Manage anxiety reaction and keep it at an optimal level.

- Reassure yourself that you are ready for the performance.
- Interpret anxiety as something that can be used constructively.
- Remind yourself to use coping techniques such as breathing awareness.
- Remain focussed on your performance goals and cut off outside distractions.

EXAMPLES

- Now, let me run through my checklist of things to do.
- I have done it in practice and rehearsal and I can do it here.
- I can meet this challenge.
- Although I feel a little nervous, this is normal and once I get onstage it will go away.
- Relax, I'm in control. Practise my breath awareness.
- Think about my performance goals.
- What is the first thing I need to concentrate on?

3. DURING THE PERFORMANCE:

OBJECTIVES

- Use coping techniques if you are becoming overly anxious.
- Have strategies or techniques for dealing with mistakes.
- Stay focussed in the present.
- Enjoy the performance.

EXAMPLES

- Keep my focus on the present and let go of the past.
- 'Oops', a mistake; let it go.
- My muscles are getting tense; drop the shoulders.
- Breathe easily.
- Focus on the tempo, dynamics etc, especially what is going right.
- Stay task relevant.

4. AFTER THE PERFORMANCE:

OBJECTIVES

- Evaluate the performance honestly, what worked and what did not. Evaluation influences how you approach your next performance.
- Accept people's praise graciously, even if you don't necessarily believe them at the time.
- Recognise that you are in a heightened emotional state.
- Acknowledge small gains, and don't belittle gradual progress.

- Get real feedback from others on your performance some time later.

EXAMPLES

- I've survived.
- I did most of the things I wanted to.
- Although it's not 100 per cent yet, I'm pleased with the progress I'm making.
- What can I learn from this performance?
- I need to allow myself time to come back to earth.
- People mean well when they praise me, and most of them are genuine.
- Next time, I'll do it even better.

Start creating your own list of standard self-talk for each of the four stages of performing so that you are fully prepared mentally for your next performance.

This chapter has concentrated on how to change some important aspects of your thinking. The next chapter looks at techniques for changing your physiological reactions.

ACTIVITY 1: DISCOVER YOUR SUBPERSONALITY TYPE
Another way to analyse your negative self-statements is to divide them into the four sub-personality styles of thinking (the Worrier, the Critic, the Victim and the Perfectionist). Most performers find they tend towards one or two of these styles. Once you have identified yours, you can then change the thinking of these dominant sub-personalities to more positive and realistic ones.

ACTIVITY 2: DEVELOPING POSITIVE SELF-TALK
To begin monitoring your self-talk, write down the typical things you think of in the four stages of performing, then experiment with converting them into more positive and realistic self-talk. To assist you in identifying those self-statements which are unhelpful, you can look for the following keywords and convert them in the ways suggested.

NEGATIVE		POSITIVE
I always	to	I often
I never	to	I rarely
I must	to	I prefer
I need	to	I want
I can't	to	I would find it difficult or I choose not to
I can never	to	in the past, I have found it difficult to

After completing this exercise, you will find you have a short list of self-statements which are uplifting and realistic, and which you can say to yourself whenever you're thinking in a negative and self-defeating way. Remember, most habits take time to break so, to change old habits, you will need to keep working on them.

3 The Relaxed Artist

*The relaxation response ... allows you a respite from
external stress of the environment and the internal stress
of your thoughts.*
Davis, Eshelman & McKay

THE AUTONOMIC NERVOUS SYSTEM

It is good to be alert and excited before a performance, and to achieve this, you need to maintain your psychological build-up to the performance. Winding down after a performance is also a skill which is useful to develop, because this allows you to recover more quickly and be fresh for your next performance. To learn how to control your build-up and to wind down, it is helpful to understand the role of the autonomic nervous system and its two parts, the sympathetic nervous system and the parasympathetic nervous system .

The autonomic nervous system controls the bodily functions that keep us alive, such as our breathing, heart, digestive system, and urinary system. These functions are all essential for life and we carry them out without thinking about it. There are two parts to the autonomic nervous system, the sympathetic and the parasympathetic nervous systems, and they each have different roles. The sympathetic nervous system is like an 'on switch' and is responsible for making us alert. It is the system that initiates the fight or flight response. The parasympathetic nervous system is like an 'off switch' and is responsible for calming us down and helping us to go to sleep. The actions of the sympathetic and parasympathetic systems are always in balance, one tending to dominate the other according to what we need to do.

How do you like to relax? When I have asked artists this question, they give a range of answers from 'I don't relax at all' to 'I meditate every day'. Often, they will mention recreational activities such as reading, watching TV, gardening, playing sport, knitting and socialising. There are different types of relaxation activities and different ones are appropriate for different purposes.

In general, recreational activities are very good for taking your mind off performing. The most effective type of relaxation for *anxiety control* is full body relaxation, because this type of relaxation works directly on activating the parasympathetic nervous system, the 'off switch'. But for general time out, activities such as the ones mentioned above are the best.

All people need both recreational and relaxation activities. These activities are great for helping artists to manage the build-up to a performance and to unwind afterwards. Relaxation exercises have been shown to reduce heart rate, breathing rate, metabolic rate, sweating, muscle tension and adrenalin secretion. Relaxation has also been shown to increase alpha brainwave patterns, which have been linked with creative thinking.

OVER-BREATHING AND BREATHING AWARENESS

The easiest and quickest form of relaxation is through the use of breathing. When artists become anxious, they are likely to over-breathe by taking faster and more shallow breaths from the chest area or the upper half of the lungs. If you put one hand on your chest and one on your abdomen, you will be able to tell whether you are breathing more from the chest or more from the lower part of the lungs. When you breathe more from the chest, your chest rises when you breathe in. When you are breathing from the lower lungs, your abdomen rises as you breathe in.

The healthiest breathing occurs when the abdomen rises more than the chest. However, when you are anxious, you are more likely to breathe from the chest. Breathing from the bottom of the lungs uses the muscle between the lungs and abdomen (the diaphragm) and breathing into the top part of the lungs uses the chest muscles.

Research has shown that breathing plays a critical part in the anxiety response.

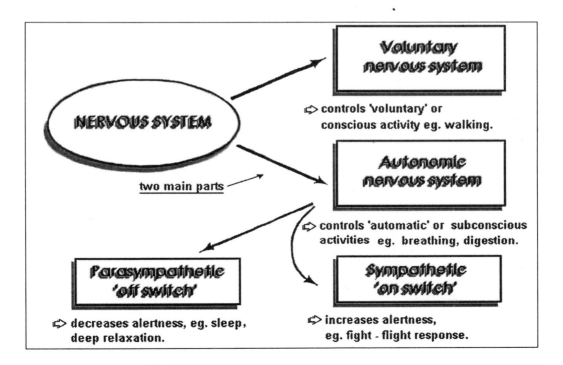

When you over-breathe, the oxygen and carbon dioxide ratio in the blood changes and can lead to many of the symptoms of anxiety, including trembling in the hands and legs. Over-breathing can also create pains in the chest because the body's natural response is to slow the breathing rate down by tightening the muscles around the chest.

Margaret was a piano player who experienced chest pains quite regularly, particularly in connection with performing. It had become so serious that she consulted her doctor about it, because she thought she might be experiencing the early signs of a heart attack. She came to one of my relaxation classes and learned the breathing relaxation exercise. She came back the next week after having practised the breathing relaxation, and told me that all her chest pains had gone and she realised they must have been from over-breathing. Of course, she was delighted with such a simple cure. I explained to her that when a person over-breathes, the muscles around the chest tighten to force the lungs to reduce the amount of air they take in.

Jenny was a dancer who had started experiencing nausea before competing. By simply practising the breathing awareness exercise before performing, she was able to reduce her nausea almost completely. I explained to Jenny that one of the effects of the fight or flight response is the shut-down of the digestive system when we feel threatened. By practising breathing awareness, she was reversing the effects of the fight or flight response and, as a consequence, she felt less threatened.

Most artists are not aware of how their breathing is related to anxiety before a performance. Even singers and wind players who use their breathing as part of their music-making do not realise how they can use it as a way of calming down. How do you tell if you are over-breathing?

SIGNS OF OVER-BREATHING

1.   Breathing too quickly — breathing is quicker than normal and consists of shallow breaths from the chest area.
2.   Sighing and yawning — taking occasional sighs (deep breaths) or continual yawning which increases your oxygen intake.
3.   Habitual over-breathing occurs when people breathe too quickly and/or deeply over a long period of time. Because it has become a habit, it is harder to notice. It may leave such people always feeling slightly apprehensive and more prone to feeling anxious when they find themselves in stressful situations.

Extreme over-breathing in a performance situation can lead to a condition called hyperventilation, where the artist feels as though she has lost control of her breathing completely. Some of the symptoms of hyperventilation include:

•   light-headedness or faintness
•   dizziness
•   quickening of the heart rate

- tingling sensations in hands, arms and feet
- dry mouth
- cold, pale hands
- a feeling of rising apprehension
- trembling of the hands and legs
- tightness or pain in the chest
- blurred vision
- headache
- feelings of panic
- a desire to escape

Using the breathing awareness exercise is a very easy way to control the physiological effects of performance anxiety. Unlike the other physiological effects of anxiety, breathing is under your conscious control and you don't need any special equipment to modify it. It can be practised anytime and anywhere, including while waiting to go on stage, and even during a performance. The research on anxiety suggests that if you keep your breathing under control, it will be impossible for you to experience the strong physiological symptoms of performance anxiety. Not only does breathing awareness produce beneficial physical effects, it also has the effect of calming the mind and allowing your thoughts to become more focussed.

Marilyn Horne, an opera singer, comments on the value of using diaphragmatic breathing not only to control the voice but to also control the physical symptoms of anxiety.

> That (breathing) will take away stage fright in two seconds. Excuse me ... that won't take the fright away, but that will take the shake away. When you start pushing on that diaphragm, that's going to start controlling your voice immediately.
>
> *Hines, 1994*

FULL BODY RELAXATION

Learning how to relax provides a general strategy for coping with stress and anxiety in daily life. It also enhances mental functions such as concentration and memory. A person who is generally calm is likely to be able to handle performance situations more comfortably because her level of anxiety will be lower to begin with.

There are many varieties of relaxation that can be practised, but they all have in common the aim of releasing muscle tension and allowing the body and mind to 'let go'. The two methods I have found consistently helpful for artists are progressive muscle relaxation (PMR) and autogenic relaxation (AR). I usually suggest that you try PMR first as this is a more active, physical type of relaxation and is easier to do if you haven't done much relaxation before. PMR follows two principles. The first is to *tense and relax* different parts of the body and notice the difference between the sensations of relaxation and tension. The second principle is to *progressively* work through the major muscle groups of the body while tensing and relaxing them. See Activity 2 for the instructions on this exercise.

Autogenic relaxation does not require any physical movement at all and is a more mental style of relaxation. Once people have become used to relaxing, they often find the Autogenic style more deeply relaxing. Autogenic Relaxation involves mentally giving your attention to a particular part of the body and then *sending the message of relaxation to it* and thinking of it *becoming warm and heavy*. Once again, you work progressively throughout the major muscle groups of the body. You can incorporate a visualisation of a peaceful and tranquil scene for one or two minutes at the end of the relaxation sequence. See Activity 2 for the instructions for this exercise.

When do you do relaxation exercises? Relaxation can be done on a regular, even daily, basis. If done this way, it will have the overall effect of reducing your stress levels. For artists, it is particularly valuable in the days and weeks leading up to a major performance, or between performances that are close together. It is during these periods that muscle tension, anxiety and agitation tend to increase. Many artists experience difficulty sleeping as a performance draws nearer, and relaxation can help with the onset of sleep, when normally there is tossing and turning and difficulty switching off thoughts.

Susan was participating in an overseas dance competition which involved performances each day over a period of a week. Normally, she found it took her a while to unwind after a performance, so it was important for her to recover quickly after each performance and be fresh for the next day. She would also usually find that she had thoughts the following day about her performance, going over and over in her mind and keeping her awake. I showed her how to do the PMR and AR exercises and gave her a cassette tape with a recording of each, so that she could have my familiar voice guiding her through the exercises. During the competition, she listened to the tape every night before going to sleep and found she was able to drop off to sleep quite easily. As a result, she found herself waking each day much more refreshed and alert than she would normally have been.

If you are performing on a regular basis, some form of relaxation is very valuable in helping you wind down after a performance and renew your mental and physical energy. Chapter 8 discusses further how relaxation fits into a pre-performance routine.

Besides progressive muscle relaxation and autogenic relaxation, any form of relaxation that acts on the parasympathetic nervous system is suitable. Other forms of relaxation that can achieve these changes include hatha yoga, tai chi, meditation, massage and float-tank sessions. Regular aerobic exercise can also have a strong relaxation effect — this will be discussed further in Chapter 6.

ACTIVITY 1: BREATHING AWARENESS

The effects of over-breathing can be counteracted by a simple technique called breathing awareness. Breathing awareness involves slowing your breathing rate down and taking in air so that the bottom of your lungs fill first, before air fills the chest area. A person needs only to take, on average, 10 to 14 breaths per minute when he is physically inactive. If your breathing rate exceeds this then you are breathing more quickly than you need to when at rest.

Check your breathing to see if you tend to breathe from the chest or from the abdomen by placing one hand on your chest and the other on your abdomen. Notice how fast or slowly you are breathing. Notice whether you are breathing in a regular way or holding your breath. Notice that as you breathe in, your chest and abdomen rise. If your chest rises more than your abdomen, your breathing needs to be deeper.

To practise the technique of breathing awareness take the following steps:

1.   Find a comfortable position either sitting or lying down. It is good the first few times to practise the exercise with your eyes closed, but once you become used to it, you can do it with your eyes open.
2.   Begin by becoming aware of your breathing and noticing how it flows in and out of your nostrils.
3.   As you breathe in, begin to feel the air going right to the bottom of the lungs. You can help this process by 'seeing' the air going to the bottom of the lungs.
4.   Allow your breath to become slow and smooth. When the breath is smooth, it will flow in and out with a steady rhythm, like waves breaking on a beach.
5.   Each time you breathe out, feel the body letting go, with your shoulders dropping and your arms becoming loose. Feel tension draining away from the whole body.
6.   After a few minutes, or longer if you prefer, return your awareness to the room and open your eyes. You might want to stretch out your arms and legs to wake up again.

To increase your proficiency in the use of breathing awareness, practise becoming aware of your breathing as you go about your normal day; for example, when walking or driving (with your eyes open of course!). You will begin to notice that your breathing changes all the time in response to your circumstances. It is important to do this general practice, as you will want to be able to switch it on quickly in performance when you need it most. I often encourage artists to incorporate breathing awareness in their practice sessions. If you are working from a musical score or choreographed piece, you can work out breathing breaks for when you particularly want to breathe freely. Breathing awareness forms part of the centering exercise discussed in Chapter 8.

ACTIVITY 2: RELAXATION
It is difficult to learn relaxation exercises from reading a book. They are best taught first hand by a teacher, either individually or in a group. Relaxation-training techniques are commonly taught by psychologists, yoga teachers and some other health

professionals, or they can be learned through relaxation or stress-management courses. There are also commercially produced relaxation tapes available, including the one accompanying this book, which are a second-best alternative. Ultimately, you want to have learned the relaxation exercises sufficiently well so that you can carry them out by yourself without the need for a teacher or a tape. For this reason I have provided verbatim transcriptions of the relaxation exercises I use (see the Appendix). You can read them through and record them on your own audio cassette, but it does take some practice to get the tempo and voice tone right.

For relaxation to be effective, it is necessary to practise it regularly in the initial stages for 15 to 20 minutes. Find a quiet place where you can lie down or sit (with back support). Get as comfortable as you can, with legs uncrossed and arms by your sides. Close your eyes.

(1) Progressive Muscle Relaxation

Tense for about five seconds and then relax for about ten seconds each part of the body listed below. Notice the difference between tension and relaxation. Repeat the procedure a second time. You can vary the muscle groups you wish to work on to suit your needs.

1. Hands — make a fist with your hands, feeling the tension growing in the hands and arms, and then let go of the tension completely by letting the fingers spread out. Repeat.
2. Arms — make a fist with your hands and bring the hands towards your shoulders, creating tension in the arms. Relax and then repeat.
3. Shoulders — shrug the shoulders up towards your ears to create tension. Relax and repeat.
4. Face — wrinkle up the face muscles to create tension. Relax and repeat.
5. Jaws — tighten the jaws to create tension. Relax and repeat.
6. Neck — press the head back against the surface it is resting on to create tension. Relax and repeat.
7. Back — arch the back by pushing out the stomach to create tension. Relax and repeat.
8. Chest — take in a deep breath and hold it for about 10 seconds to create tension. Relax and repeat.
9. Stomach — tighten the muscles of the stomach to create tension. Relax and repeat.
10. Legs — stretch out the legs and lift them up a little to create tension. Relax and repeat.
11. Now give your attention to your whole body, allowing it to become absorbed in the overall feeling of relaxation.
12. When you are ready, allow your attention to slowly return to the room and open your eyes.

(2) Autogenic Relaxation

This exercise works progressively through different parts of the body. As you focus on each part of the body, think of it becoming more and more relaxed and then becoming warm and heavy. As you breathe out, feel the tension being released from that part of the body.

Try the following sequence of body parts. Arms: left hand, left forearm, left upper arm, left shoulder, right hand, right forearm, right upper arm, right shoulder. Legs: left foot, left calf, left thigh, right foot, right calf, right thigh. Torso: stomach, chest, back, buttocks. Head: neck, face, jaw, lips, eyes, scalp.

Feel a wave of relaxation pass down the whole body and enjoy the overall feeling of relaxation for a few minutes. When you are ready, allow your attention to slowly return to the room and open your eyes.

4 Focussing Your Attention On What Matters

A calm mind and clear vision are attained in a quiet body, and only the quiet and focusing mind can perceive the ticking of a clock or produce an exquisite tone on a musical instrument.

William and Constance Starr in Kimball, Petersen & Johnson, 1990

How well do you concentrate before going on stage and during the performance? How well do you concentrate during practice and rehearsals? If you are like most artists, you sometimes find it difficult to concentrate in these situations. Perhaps you are aware that you are distracted by what is going on around you, perhaps you feel tense, or perhaps you are preoccupied with negative thoughts about the performance. Perhaps you have made a mistake during the performance and the memory of it is playing on your mind. Perhaps you feel tired or not terribly enthusiastic, or perhaps you have just had some good or bad news and you are finding it difficult to focus fully on your performance. It is quite normal to experience some or all of these things some of the time.

This chapter explains how you can maintain full concentration even when you are distracted by something that is irrelevant to performing. In everyday language, we talk about being able to concentrate, but I prefer to call it focussed attention. Concentration is a word that often conjures up the idea of having to make an effort. But being able to concentrate does not necessarily require effort, rather, it is a matter of simply shifting your attention to focus on what matters.

> He [Louis Armstrong] also taught me by example that the key to music, the key to life, is concentration.
>
> *Bobby Hackett in Kimball, Petersen & Johnson, 1990*

FINDING YOUR PET IN THE DARK

Imagine it is dark and you are at home looking for your pet dog or cat that hasn't shown up at the end of the day for its dinner. You walk out into the garden looking for it with a torch. Notice that as you shine your torch towards where you think your pet might be, you are illuminating that part of the garden, but that the other parts of the garden are in darkness. If you want to see these parts of the garden you simply shine your torch onto these areas. At any one time, you are able to illuminate only one part of your garden to the exclusion of the rest.

Notice that whatever you choose to shine your torch on, it gives out exactly the same amount of light. Focussing your attention is like shining your torch. You have a certain amount of attention that you can give to something at any one moment and it is a matter of directing your attention onto the aspect that is important to you. 'Concentrating hard' on something is simply *narrowing* your attention and focussing it on a particular point. This does not need to be an effort.

THE DIFFERENT TYPES OF ATTENTION

There are different ways to focus attention. Some torches allow you to widen or narrow the beam of light so that you can broaden or narrow your field of view. Because the torch gives out the same amount of light every time, when you broaden the beam of light, it becomes less intense while it illuminates a greater area. When you narrow the beam of light, it becomes more intense and illuminates a smaller area.

This also applies to your attention. If you are in the mountains and you look out across a beautiful view of a valley, your attention is very broad because you are taking in the view of the whole valley. If you were to stoop down and examine a small flower near your feet, your attention would be very narrow but more intense.

Another way to focus your attention is inside or outside yourself. When you are looking out across the view of the valley or down at the plant, your attention is focussed outside of yourself; that is, on external objects. If you were to become aware of your body feeling cold because of a sharp wind blowing, then your attention would be focussed inside yourself; that is, on your physical sensations of cold. You would also be focussed internally if you became aware of a feeling of peace and calm inspired by the view; that is, on your emotional response.

ATTENTION AND PERFORMING

Let's look now at attention in the performance context. During the lead-up to a performance, you tend to be focussed on many things to do with the performance — learning your lines, songs, rehearsals, costumes, instruments, other artists, organising your life around rehearsals, publicity, eating, sleeping, socialising and so on. There are limitless things that can be mentally focussed upon, so your attention will usually be broad at this time. Sometimes it will be narrow, such as when you are practising. When you are rehearsing, your attention will alternate between being internal and external. It will be external when you are focussed on the director, conductor, or other artists, and it will be internal when you are focussed on your thoughts and on what you are doing.

INTERNAL AND EXTERNAL FOCUS

INTERNAL	EXTERNAL
Think of the tempo for the opening bars.	What does the conductor want here?
Remember to use the right accent with this speech.	Watch out for my cue.
Feel the rising anger in this dialogue.	Listen to the mood of the music.
Think of being startled for this sequence.	Notice anger on the other dancers' faces.
Feel the vibration of the drumming.	Feel the enthusiasm coming from the audience.

As you approach a performance, your attention will generally go from the broad to the narrow.

> You are creating something within the stage, and the concentration has to be total on what you're doing, all the way through. You can't let up for a minute.
>
> *Moira Shearer, ballet dancer, in Newman, 1992*

FOCUS ON THE ARTIST, THE AUDIENCE AND THE PERFORMANCE PROCESS

During a performance, there are three possible areas to focus your attention on: yourself, the audience or the performance process. The performance process is what you are actually doing and can include the music, choreography, script, or any other creative aspect of the performance.

Focussing on yourself during a performance may or may not be helpful, depending on how you do it. It is helpful to focus on yourself in a positive way, such as checking tension in the body, using breathing awareness, or giving yourself positive self-talk. If you are focussing on yourself with negative self-talk, then this is unhelpful and will only lead to anxiety. Focussing on the audience is unhelpful if you are thinking about how the audience is evaluating you, or if you are simply being aware of how it is looking at you. Focussing on the performance process is the most constructive, because this will preclude your thinking about the audience, or being overly focussed on yourself, and so it will create the greatest amount of mental freedom in your performing. The less self-conscious an artist appears to the audience, the more likely the audience will see past the artist and become involved in the performance itself. One musician (a violinist) I interviewed was expressing a similar view to this when he said: 'I've tried to get away from the focus on myself ... where I cease to exist as an artist, and "it", the music, is the most important ... to make the music become alive and assume its own identity is the most important thing.'

THOUGHTS, EMOTIONS AND KINAESTHETIC SENSATIONS

There are three types of mental processes we can focus on: thoughts, emotions and kinaesthetic sensations. Thoughts are like little conversations we have with ourselves about what we are doing and what is going on around us. We looked at the idea of negative and positive self-talk, which are examples of thoughts, in Chapter 2. Emotions describe feelings we are experiencing. An artist may experience emotions that are related to the specific performance of a song or role, for example, or she may experience emotions that are related to how she is feeling in general.

Kinaesthetic sensations are knowing what your body is experiencing in a physical sense. If you close your eyes, raise your arm above your head and then lower it, how is it you know where your arm is even when you can't see it? When you move across a stage, how do you know where to move your feet without tripping up? The neuromuscular system of the body is in constant communication, which lets you know what physical sensations you are experiencing and how you are moving.

The artist can be focussed at any one time on a thought, emotion, or kinaesthetic sensation. These are all examples of internal focus and all will be relevant for a performance depending upon what the artist needs to be doing.

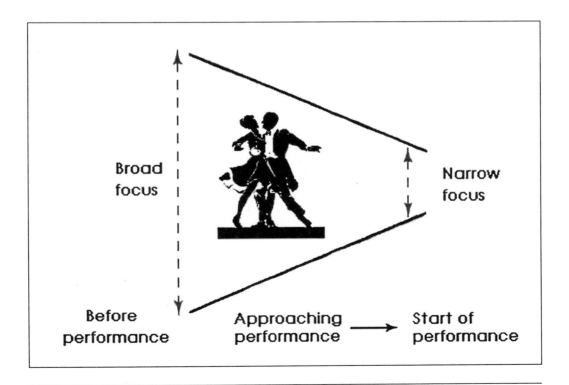

EXPERIMENTING WITH YOUR FOCUS

Artists often have difficulty learning how to shift their attention easily from the inside to the outside and from the broad to the narrow, and knowing when to do this. Different types of attention are required at different times. You can begin developing this skill at any instant by asking yourself 'What am I focussing on now?' and then experimenting by shifting your focus to something else. You'll begin to notice that in the same situation, there is a number of different things you could be focussed on. By practising this exercise over and over again in any situation related to performing, you will increase your skill at shifting easily from internal to external, and from broad to narrow and vice versa.

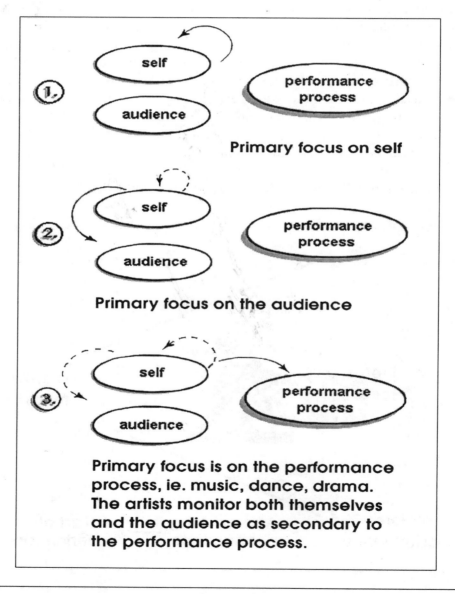

Primary focus on self

Primary focus on the audience

Primary focus is on the performance process, ie. music, dance, drama. The artists monitor both themselves and the audience as secondary to the performance process.

TASK-RELEVANT FOCUS

Now that you are more aware of what you are focussing on, how do you know if you are focussing on the right thing? It's easy for artists to find themselves becoming distracted by all that is going on around them before a performance, or by thoughts which are not relevant to the performance. Some professional artists say that while they are performing, they sometimes catch themselves thinking irrelevant things such as 'What will I be having for dinner tonight?' or 'What shopping do I need to do?' Alternatively, others will be having thoughts like 'What's so and so in the audience thinking about me?' or 'The acoustics are bad here' or 'I feel cold and stiff'. These are all thoughts which don't assist you in performance because they are irrelevant to the task of performing at that time and reduce your focus on the performance.

What is the best thing to be thinking about while you are performing and while you are preparing to perform? You can make a useful distinction between thoughts that are on factors which don't assist your performance (task-irrelevant) and thoughts that are on the process of performing (task-relevant). A task-irrelevant thought is one that has nothing to do with your performance at the time; for example 'What will I have for dinner tonight?'. A task-relevant thought is one that has its focus on aspects that are helpful to the performance; for example 'At this point, I want to move with the gliding motion of a swan'.

One of the greatest performance pressures brought to bear on people in contemporary society must surely be that of an Olympic athlete waiting to compete in an event. In this instance the athlete could be thinking about all his compatriots watching him, watching the crowd around him, or thinking about how good his opponents are and what it would mean to win a gold medal. However, all these thoughts serve only to create a mental burden, and have no relevance to how he runs his race at that moment. These aspects may be of interest to him well before the race or after it, but have no relevance immediately before it or during it. The thoughts that will help the athlete most are thoughts about the race plan and staying focussed on implementing it. The research evidence in sports psychology indicates that athletes perform at their best when they are not concentrating on the outcome of their event or peripheral things happening around them while they are competing, but rather on what they actually need to be doing during the event.

Comedian Wendy Harmer describes the behind the scenes atmosphere at a comedy festival, a good example of how not to remain focussed.

> It's just vile you have 40 anxious comedians, all nervous about whether they're going to be funny or not, standing around asking, 'Am I on? Am I on now? When am I on?'. When they're not on, they're looking at the monitor bitching about everybody else's act. 'Hang on a minute, that's my line,' they say. Or 'I remember that joke from '73'.

The Australian, *20 April 1994*

A concert pianist on an international tour told me of how a very unexpected thing happened in his first concert. He had gone to the Sydney Opera House to practise the day before his concert to familiarise himself with the piano and the acoustics of the hall. However, when he began playing the following evening, he found to his horror that the piano sounded quite different from the way it had during his practice session. Although this was very unsettling at first, he recovered his mental focus and played his way through the remainder of the concert. Although the audience enjoyed his performance, he felt he did not play as well as he could have. After the concert, he told the stage manager about his experience and found out that changes had been made to the acoustic baffling over the stage, which had affected the sound of the piano. The pianist expressed his disapproval to the stage manager for making such changes without warning him. Things were put right for the repeat performance a few evenings later and he said the performance went much better when the sound was what he was expecting.

It's easy to become caught up in the distractions around you before performing, but it is to your advantage to tune out from these distractions and to think only about what you need to do to complete your performance successfully. This means not thinking about what your teacher, family, peers or audience expects of you, what's going on backstage around you or any other potential distractions. Artists at auditions, competing in eisteddfods or competitions, may find themselves backstage with their 'opponents', sometimes having to perform the same piece. This can be particularly distracting. In a situation like this, it is best not to be around the other competitors. Avoid seeing and hearing, as much as possible, what they are doing before you perform. Doing this will help you stay task-relevant in your focus for *your* performance.

What do you do if you find yourself habitually being task-irrelevant in your thinking? (See Chapter 8 for more details on a pre-performance routine.) There is a technique that is very useful.

1.   Notice when your mind is thinking something that is task-irrelevant.
2.   Ask yourself this question: 'What is the most helpful thing for me to be focussed on right now?' Choose an alternative thought that is task-relevant.
3.   Practise thinking this whenever a task-irrelevant thought comes to mind.

When you are preparing to perform, it would be relevant to be thinking about your performance goals (see Chapter 7), your breathing, imagery that helps you get into the mood of your performance, noticing tension in the body and relaxing, marking out the first steps you need to dance, giving yourself positive self-talk, and so on. While you are performing, it is relevant to be thinking about the notes you are playing, the words you are speaking, the artistic dynamics of what you are doing, how you need to interact with the other artists on the stage, or listening to the timing of the music, your body posture or movement, and technical aspects such as the sound of your voice. When you are not accustomed to using task-relevant thinking, it can take some practice to get your thoughts going in this direction. However, by simply being aware of when you are thinking task-irrelevant thoughts, you will be amazed at how easy it can be to think in a more task-relevant way, and how this produces much better results in your performances.

Things happen in a performance which you can't foresee, and the objective in these circumstances is to remain as task-relevant in your focus as possible. Having such a focus will pull you through, even in very trying performance conditions.

HOW DO I DEAL WITH MISTAKES ?

Something that every artist has to deal with is making mistakes. It is common for an artist, even a seasoned professional, to make a mistake in a performance. A mistake can range from a serious memory lapse to not achieving a particular dynamic emphasis in part of the performance. A mistake in performance is the worst kind of distraction for the artist and can lead to task-irrelevant thinking. The artist usually thinks the mistake he has made is much more obvious to the audience than is actually the case. There may be a dancer, musician or actor in the audience who has sufficient technical knowledge to notice if a mistake has been made, but the average audience member is not usually aware of it. But, if the audience does become aware of the mistake, it is usually because the artist makes it obvious by his facial expressions or behaviour.

Caroline O'Connor, who performed in *West Side Story*, recalls a performance when she was playing the character Anita. 'All of a sudden, I momentarily blanked out. It was only for a few seconds but inevitably it felt like an hour. Perhaps I was too excited, but for whatever reason, I started doing some Irish dancing.' (The *Australian*, 25–26 February, 1995.)

Groucho Marx describes an early incident in the professional career of the Marx brothers when they were known as the Nightingales. They were given their first big break when they were invited to perform with a soprano in an evening variety show after one of the scheduled acts had failed to arrive.

> Well, the orchestra struck up the introduction, a thrilling sound; the soprano walked on the stage alone, to sing the verse of *Love Me and the World is Mine*. Gummo and I, slickly attired in white yachting outfits, with artificial flowers in our lapels, marched in from opposite sides of the stage to join in the chorus with our trick harmonies and barber-shop chords which we thought were pretty hot. The chorus of *Love Me and the World is Mine* jumps from B flat to C, and the soprano inadvertently leaped to E flat. And she leaped alone, for Gummo and I had rehearsed the chorus in C, and no soprano was going to get us to change. The audience laughed more at our comic nervousness than at the botching of the song and we went on singing, hoping that a bolt of lightening would appear to strike us all dead. Never before had I known such anguish. A miserable experience ... a happy memory.
>
> *Groucho Marx, 1995.*

I've been imitated so well I've heard people copy my mistakes.
Jimi Hendrix guitarist and rock musician, in Kohut & Kohut ,1994.

Artists who are anxious about performing focus excessively on their mistakes and not on the other aspects of their performance that are going well for them. One way to help fix this problem is to make a recording of your performance so that you can hear or view it a few days later. After a few days, you will have settled down and will be able to relive your performance more as an audience member rather than as the performer. Alternatively, you can ask for the opinion of someone you respect and trust and who will be at the performance to give you honest feedback about how you went. Both these methods will help you get the performance in perspective, both the good and the bad aspects.

In summary, there are several points to remember when dealing with mistakes:

1. Put the mistakes in perspective and acknowledge what went well in the performance and what the overall effect was like — do the mistakes really ruin the whole performance? Treat mistakes you make as pointers to what needs further work.
2. Remember that you will notice your mistakes much more than the audience does, so there is no need to accentuate them.
3. Leave mistakes in the past during a performance and stay focussed on the present, even though you might be mad at yourself at the time.
4. When you make a mistake during a performance, immediately become task focussed. Bring yourself back to the rhythm of the music, the emotion of your role, the kinaesthetic feel of your movement etc.
5. You can also refocus using keywords and imagery, which are discussed in Chapter 5.

STAYING IN THE PRESENT

Generally we are able to hold about seven bits of information in our short-term memory at once, for example a seven digit telephone number. When you are performing, you are fully occupied mentally, unless you are doing something very easy or something you can do 'on automatic pilot'. This means you can attend to only about seven aspects of your performance at any one time. When you make a mistake and you keep thinking about it (that's one bit of information), then you have sufficient attention left to think of six other things. If you make another mistake and you keep thinking about this one as well as the first mistake you made, then you can only think of about five things in the present. Because you now have less attention focussed on your immediate performance, it becomes more likely that you will make further mistakes, and so on. Many artists would have experienced the domino effect that making one initial mistake can have in producing others. The lesson from this is to let go of mistakes when they happen, leave them in the past where they belong, and stay focussed on what you are doing *now*. If you do this you'll always be able to remain focussed on seven bits of information. You can analyse how you went wrong in a performance after it is over. If you want to be mad with yourself, do it then.

Paul was a professional actor who had recently returned to acting after a period of time working as a director. At the time he consulted me he was acting in a play in which he was not the director. During rehearsals he was finding it difficult to 'get into' his role because he was distracted by internal dialogue about how he would have directed the play. This was exacerbated further because his ideas of how best to direct the play differed in many ways from those of the appointed director. In helping Paul with this difficulty, we discussed the appropriate self-talk he could use to help himself stay focussed in the present and on his role as a actor. I also asked Paul to recall a previous role in which he had felt fully involved as an actor, which he was able to do easily. Re-experiencing the memory of this role allowed him to re-engage with the acting experience. Paul then used the images from this role to help him in his mental preparation for his present role. As a result, he was able to switch off the internal dialogue about directing and he began to feel a new freedom in his acting.

ACTIVITY 1: TASK-RELEVANT FOCUS

Start to notice when your thoughts, emotions or kinaesthetic sense are task-relevant and when they are not. You have to build this awareness of your mental focus for yourself. No-one else can do it for you. Building this awareness will give you choices about what you give your attention to. You will start to notice habits in the way you operate mentally. If the answer to the question, 'Is what I am focussed on now helping me to perform or prepare to perform?', is yes, then this mental focus is task-relevant. If the mental focus is not helping your performance or is distracting, then it is task-irrelevant. Try practising task-relevant focus when you are in practice and rehearsals and not just when performing.

ACTIVITY 2: HANDLING MISTAKES

Start to become aware of how you react when you make a mistake, what thoughts you have and how you respond emotionally and physically. Practise putting thoughts or feelings about a mistake in the past, so you can stay focussed on the present. You can analyse your mistakes after the performance.

ACTIVITY 3: GAINING FEEDBACK

Record some of your practice sessions and performances so that you are able to listen to them on audio tape or watch them on video tape afterwards, and assess them as if you were an audience member. Ask people you respect for their feedback about your live performances so that you are getting someone else's perspective on your performance. You can also brief them to look out for a particular aspect of your performance which you feel is suspect. Doing these things helps you to assess how you are going.

ACTIVITY 4: FOCUSSED ATTENTION

The main purpose of focussing your attention is to be able to focus on the present and on the things that are relevant to your performance. One way to improve your ability to do this is by practising with exercises, such as the following one.

Look at a wall or space that is reasonably interesting. Notice aspects of the wall or space, such as colours, shapes, textures, shadows, interesting features and so on. Then pick out one point on the wall or space and fix your attention on it without moving your eyes away from it. Do this for about 30 seconds. What did you notice as you did this? One thing that people often experience is that the background fades so that they no longer notice it, while the point they are focussing on seems to become brighter and more intense. Whatever your experience, the main purpose of the activity is to see how, when you narrow your mental focus on a point, peripheral things become less distracting and relevant things become more obvious. You can also do this exercise with sound by closing your eyes and listening to sounds in your environment, then picking out one sound and focussing on this.

5 Mental Rehearsal: The Armchair Method of Performing

Quality mental imagery, combined with quality physical practice, increases your overall effectiveness and brings you closer to your dreams.
Terry Orlick, 1990

THE MENTAL PERFORMANCE

Have you ever found yourself going through a performance in your mind without actually doing it physically? Perhaps you were singing a song, seeing yourself completing a dance routine or imagining the audience's response to one of your jokes. If you have done any of these things, then you were mentally rehearsing your performance. You may not have given much importance to this activity at the time because you thought of it as a casual, unplanned activity. But, when you mentally rehearse your performance, you are using mental imagery, which is a very powerful technique for improving your ability to perform well.

During my research with professional musicians, I found that they would often 'hear' the music they were preparing for their next performance in their heads. One orchestral conductor described how he would be rehearsing his next performance in his head, when he was on a bus or walking. An opera singer described how she would go through in her mind all the stage movements of the opera she was working on, as part of her normal preparation. Mental-rehearsal activities such as these are an important strategy in helping artists prepare themselves for performance.

Research in the field of sports psychology has shown that the use of mental imagery helps athletes to perform better in competition. Terry Orlick, a sports psychologist who has worked with many Olympic athletes, says:

> The world's best athletes have extremely well-developed imagery skills. They use imagery daily to prepare themselves to get what they want out of training, to perfect skills within training sessions, to make technical corrections, to imagine themselves succeeding in competition, and to strengthen their belief in their capacity to achieve their ultimate goal.
>
> *Orlick, 1990*

While in hospital for an eye operation, ballet dancer Alicia Alonso used mental imagery in her preparation for her first role in *Giselle* by drawing on her past observations of performances of the ballet.

> I didn't realise in those days that I was, in my mind, filing all that I was looking at. I realised it in later years, when I was lying in bed without being able to dance. Then I began to study this ballet; I went through my file of it. I began to look inside of me and think: This part, this person used to do very beautifully. This other part, I like this, this, this.' I started to go through all the richness of what I had seen, and then I started to make it completely my own *Giselle* from my files of experience and my own taste ... When I was lying in bed, I was going through everything I remembered, and I became an audience: I sat in front, and I was watching the performance. And when I forgot anything, whether someone comes from the left or from the right, then I do it on my fingers and try to ask, 'Wasn't this person on from the left when Hilarion was coming from here? When he was going out, wasn't the other coming in?' I went through little things, so I wouldn't be able to forget.
>
> *Newman, 1992*

Although only a small amount of scientific research has been conducted on the effectiveness of mental rehearsal in the performing arts, this research also supports the idea that mental rehearsal is useful. A research study with trombone players compared one group who only physically practised a piece of music with a second group who only mentally practised the music and with a third group who did a combination of physical and mental practice. All three groups practised the piece of music for the same length of time each day but in their three different ways. At the end of the study period, the group that combined both physical and mental practice was able to perform the piece better than the other two groups.

Mental rehearsal involves creating in your mind an image of yourself going through your performance, or parts of it, without actually physically doing so. This image includes all senses — visual, auditory, smell, taste and kinaesthetic, as well as emotions. For most artists, the visual, auditory, kinaesthetic and emotional aspects are likely to be the most important. For example, a dancer who is marking out his steps in physical practice might 'see' himself completing these steps without actually doing them. An actor might 'hear' herself speaking her lines while 'seeing' and feeling the associated stage movements. A singer might feel the emotion of the song he is 'singing' in his head.

The exact reason for the effectiveness of mental rehearsal has not yet been established. It appears mental rehearsal creates psychophysiological patterns in the body that prepare the artist to carry out the physical actions in reality. Research has found that when a person imagines themselves performing a particular action, muscular activity increases in the muscle groups that would normally be required to perform this activity. Furthermore, it has been found that brain wave patterns change when a person engages in mental imagery, depending upon the type of imagery being used, for example, visual or kinaesthetic.

Some artists find that when they visualise a performance, they see the scenes from 'inside' their body looking out, while others see the scenes from 'outside' their body as though they were watching themselves in a film, or as the audience might see them. Both ways are effective, although seeing from the 'inside' can give a greater feeling of involvement. When you imagine performance scenes, it is most effective if you feel you are really there. This means imagining all the sights, sounds, smells, sense of touch and feelings that would be present if you were performing in reality.

An advantage of mental rehearsal over physical rehearsal is that you can rehearse without becoming physically tired. This is a big advantage when you are close to a performance and want to maintain your energy level. Mental rehearsal is especially useful when your physical practice is restricted due to injury, or if you have limited access to the venue for rehearsals when on tour.

The other advantage of mental rehearsal is that you can train yourself to complete a performance perfectly even when you're still not able to do it perfectly in reality. It can be used to enhance your memory of words, music or steps without having to go through them physically.

Artists can use mental rehearsal in three main ways: to build self-confidence, reduce anxiety, and increase skill development.

BUILDING CONFIDENCE

If you are like most artists, there is at least one performance you feel you did really well. This would be an occasion when you felt things had really worked out for you, and it felt a joy to perform. If you visualise that performance in your mind, you will be able to remember what happened, how you felt, what thoughts you had, how others reacted to the performance and what you thought about the performance as a whole. You will probably remember that while you were performing, you experienced a sense of self-confidence. You can take the feeling of confidence from this performance into your next one by bringing up the memory of that good performance before you go on.

If you find you have negative images of yourself about performing, then you can replace them with positive images by imagining a past performance you did well in. Another way you can do this is to think of an artist you admire and imagine you are that artist. When you do this, you will start to take on his or her qualities and these will be expressed in reality.

'It's called "Fake it 'til you make it". For the longest time, I pretended I was George Harrison, or Mick Jagger, or Keith Richards, or "Pinetop" Perkins when I played the piano. From the very beginning: "Jeez, I can sing a song better than that!" I was pretending. Kids do it. And I did it. And it worked' (Steven Tyler, member of the rock band *Aerosmith,* quoted in Kohut & Kohut, 1994).

A young trumpet player told me she was not playing as well as she knew she could. Her teacher had told her she was not breathing effectively while playing and this was making her sound on the trumpet too thin. I suspected her problem might be due to muscle tension around the ribcage, which was restricting her breathing. I asked her to play a short excerpt from some music she had with her. After finishing the piece, she said she had felt short of breath while playing. I asked her to remember a past performance which had gone really well for her and in which she did not have this breathing problem. She remembered a solo performance she had given for a music competition. She described walking out onto the stage and as she was raising the trumpet to her lips to begin playing, she noticed a man sitting alone in the dress-circle seats at the back of the concert hall. He leaned forward with an intent expression on his face and she immediately felt he was very interested in her playing. As she played, she imagined sending out her sound to him, right to the back of the hall. I asked her to play her short excerpt again, while bringing back the image of this moment in her mind. After she finished playing this time, she said she had not experienced a breathing problem and her sound had greatly improved. What had been happening with this trumpeter was that her self-image had become constricted, and this had caused a tightening in the chest and restriction in her breathing. The more she played with this self-image, the more her poor results reinforced this view of herself. By holding a mental picture of a time when this had not been the case, she was able to bypass the negative self-talk and be her natural self.

REDUCING ANXIETY

One way to reduce anxiety before performing is to imagine yourself completing the ideal performance while being in a relaxed state. The principle behind this is that you will begin to associate your performance with being in a state of relaxation. It is important when doing this to see yourself performing in the ideal way that you would like the performance to go. The reason for this is that, through imagery, you are training the body to carry out those actions you mentally see yourself doing. If you train the body to act in a way that is not ideal, you are training it to achieve this outcome.

An easy way to become relaxed for this technique is to use the breath awareness method. (You could also use a full body relaxation or some other method; see Chapter 3.) Then imagine yourself on the day before your performance feeling excited, prepared and organised. Visualise yourself waking up the day of the performance feeling in just the frame of mind you want to be in and going through the pre-performance routine you have planned (see Chapter 8). Imagine yourself arriving at the performance venue in good time, familiarising yourself with the venue and imagining the other people you would expect to see there. Then imagine yourself waiting to go on stage feeling excited, focussed and in control. Next, imagine yourself going on stage and completing your performance in the ideal way you would like it to go. If you find at any point that you make a mistake, or something unexpected happens to temporarily throw you, then see yourself coping well with this. Finally, see yourself completing the performance successfully, coming off stage feeling euphoric and receiving a great ovation from the audience.

You might have some difficulty imagining yourself performing successfully at first, but this will become easier with practice. If you use mental rehearsal to build confidence or to reduce anxiety, it is not important that you imagine the performance taking the same length of time as it would in reality (real time): you can make it much shorter.

One professional jazz violinist told me how he particularly used mental rehearsal for television work because this was when he experienced the most anxiety in performing. 'If I had to do a television show, I'd imagine myself surrounded by cameras and lights and microphones and people standing around. I try to have a picture in my mind to psyche myself up and I'll think about that much more perhaps than what I'm going to play.'

SKILL DEVELOPMENT

The purpose of skill development is to refine old skills or gain new ones. These might be technical or artistic, such as working on dance technique, achieving certain sound qualities in the voice, or mastering a particularly difficult passage of music.

Opera singer Dame Joan Sutherland, when talking about the mental aspects of singing, said 'Sounds don't just happen. You have to have the idea of them in your mind before giving voice to them'. It is essential for the musician to be able to hear the exact sound she wants to make, or for the dancer to see and feel in his mind the exact movements he wants to achieve. They need to do this before they can really achieve them in practice, because it is the mind that tells the body what to do. Remember, each time you mentally rehearse a skill, you are developing psychophysiological patterns in the body which will help you achieve the skill in reality.

Because of the stage movements required by dancers, actors and music theatre singers, it is necessary to mentally rehearse in the visual, as well as in the auditory medium. For musicians, 'hearing' the sounds of the music they want to make is the most important aspect of mental rehearsal, together with the kinaesthetic 'feel' of moving arm and hand muscles for making the music. It helps to feel the body and the muscles moving, in synchrony with your mental image. Such movement helps you to develop the psychophysiological patterns more quickly. You may want to mentally rehearse in a standing position if this allows you to move in a way that is more appropriate for what you are rehearsing.

If your performance is a long one, it will not be possible to rehearse the whole performance in one mental practice session, so break it down into smaller sections or sequences. If you are rehearsing a sequence, rehearse the complete sequence and not just part of it.

> Ted was an opera singer who was having difficulty with the phrasing of a particularly difficult passage which required an octave leap in the middle of it. I asked him to describe the profile of the passage to me. As he did so, an image came to my mind of a bird in flight following the same 'flight path' as the passage of notes the singer was describing. When the passage came to the octave leap, I had the mental image of the bird simply tilting its wings upwards, so that it rose up suddenly and effortlessly against the breeze. I described this image to Ted, who later used it while practising this passage and reported being able to make the octave leap without any hesitation. This demonstrated that the difficulty Ted had been having previously, was not because he couldn't technically sing the passage, but because he didn't believe he could sing it easily. By taking his mental focus off this belief and putting it on to a visual image that supported his singing, he was able to achieve what he wanted easily.

Always imagine yourself completing your performance, or performance sequence, successfully, because if you rehearse yourself making errors, then you will train those errors into the body. In using mental rehearsal for skill development, it is important to rehearse it in real time. This is because you are training your neuromuscular system in a very precise way to reproduce physically, exactly what is occurring mentally.

There are many examples of how effective mental rehearsal can be for maintaining and developing a skill, such as prisoners of war who reportedly maintained skills during imprisonment. One such true story is of an American pilot who was imprisoned for some years in North Vietnam during the Vietnam War. Despite the fact that his health deteriorated during this time, he imagined himself playing eighteen holes of golf every day on his mental golf course. When he was released after the war, one of his first requests was to play a game of golf, and to everyone's amazement, he played superbly, considering his poor physical condition.

> Maryanne, a classical guitar student who was preparing for a major exam, consulted me because she was worried she wouldn't be able to play her pieces from memory. I suggested she put some time aside, several times each week, to read through her music scores, while hearing the music in her head sounding just the way she wanted it to. She was not to play her instrument while doing this. She followed this advice and spent several mornings each week in her favourite coffee shop reading through her scores in this way. It proved to be an excellent strategy for improving her memory.

ACTIVITY 1: BUILDING SELF-CONFIDENCE

1.   Remember a time when you performed really well and recall the circumstances of that occasion. Particularly remember how you felt emotionally and physically.

Use the memory of this occasion to relive those feelings and sensations you experienced then. Practise bringing this image to mind before your practice and rehearsal sessions, and then try before a real performance. Notice what differences it makes to your playing.

2. You can also experiment by recalling different images that are appropriate to specific performances. It could be a visual image that reflects the mood of the piece you are performing, or an image that gives you the physical sensations that help you reproduce the desired qualities in your performance. For example, I worked with a dancer who held the image in her mind of a particular flower which, to her, conveyed the quality of movement and energy she wanted to portray in her performance.

3. Bring to mind an image of a favourite artist or someone you admire who exhibits qualities that you would like to achieve in your performances. This is the 'fake it 'til you make it' idea. Simply practise becoming that person and acting as if you were. Notice what effects this has on your confidence. Cary Grant, as a budding 15-year-old actor, spent many hours simply observing how his heroes acted. 'At each theatre I carefully watched the celebrated headline artists from the wings, and grew to respect the diligence it took to acquire such expert timing and unaffected confidence, the amount of effort that resulted in such effortlessness.' (Fowles, 1992)

ACTIVITY 2: REDUCING ANXIETY

Mentally rehearse your next performance while in a relaxed state. Remember to make it go just the way you want it to. On the actual day of the performance, not everything will go exactly as you imagined it, so learn to expect the unexpected. Remember that while you may not have control of what happens around you, you do have control of yourself. Mental rehearsal of your performance while in a relaxed state will go a long way to helping you achieve self-control. It helps if you are familiar with the performance venue, so visit it beforehand if you can. You can even do some mental rehearsal of the performance while at the venue itself.

ACTIVITY 3: INCREASING SKILL

Mentally rehearse specific aspects of your performance you want to make more consistent, such as a difficult passage, a dance sequence, or a scene you feel awkward with. You can also mentally rehearse your whole performance in stages if necessary. Remember to rehearse it in real time, while imagining, as realistically as possible, that you are actually in the performance. The best time to do mental rehearsal is when you have some quiet time to yourself. This can be time you set aside during the day or it can be time when you are not mentally occupied, such as on public transport or walking.

6 The Healthy Artist

Whenever I feel like exercise, I lie down until the
feeling passes.
Robert Maynard Hutchins

Have you noticed that some days you feel tired or lethargic and are unable to apply yourself to performing as easily as usual? Have you found that sometimes you feel totally exhausted after performing and it seems to take days before you fully recover your energy levels? If you have experienced occasions like this, it is possible that you have been affected by factors influencing your level of physical well-being.

Although this book focusses chiefly on mental techniques for enhancing performance, the area of physical influences cannot be excluded, because they have such a large impact on our mental state. An artist in good physical health is less likely to experience illness which could interfere with performing and will manage stress more easily. In addition, good physical well-being contributes to the artist's overall level of energy and enthusiasm.

FOOD AND DRINK

> Clean living keeps me in shape. Righteous thoughts are my secret. And New Orleans home cooking.
>
> *Fats Domino in Kimball, Petersen & Johnson, 1990.*

Performing places physical demands on the body. If your body is well nourished and in good physical shape, you will handle these demands comfortably. When under the stress of performing, the body has increased metabolic needs. The increase in metabolic rate requires more B complex vitamins and increases protein use, which in turn requires more calcium in the diet. The need for other vitamins can also increase. In some cases, it may be good to take dietary supplements such as vitamins, although many nutritionists say this is not necessary when a person is following a well-balanced diet. There is plenty of information available on the make-up of the well-balanced diet, so I will not go into it here.

However there are some food concerns which have implications for artists. An unhealthy tendency in Western society is to eat too many fats and simple carbohydrates (sugars). Fats are found in red meats, dairy products, chocolate, cakes, sauces and many processed snack foods. The simple carbohydrates are found in sugar, honey, sweets, soft drinks, ice-creams and cakes. Artists are not particularly different from the general population in their dietary habits, so there is probably just as much need for them to reduce their intake of fats and simple carbohydrates as there is in the general population.

Another tendency in the Western diet is not to eat enough of the complex carbohydrates, which includes bread, pasta, brown rice, potatoes, oatmeal, beans, fruit and vegetables. These foods are more nutritious and help to maintain a stable body weight. They also provide a slower and more continuous release of energy than the simple carbohydrates, which provide a quick source of energy. The disadvantage of sugary foods as an energy source is that they cause the blood-sugar level to rise suddenly. This only lasts for a short time and eventually leads to a drop in energy levels.

Before performing, it is better to eat complex carbohydrate foods, because these foods will give you a sustained release of energy, avoiding strong energy swings. An additional benefit of the complex carbohydrates is that you are less likely to gain weight than you would by eating simple carbohydrates.

The most healthy drink to have in large quantities is water. The recommended daily intake of water varies according to body weight; for example a person weighing 65 kilograms will need up to six glasses of water per day. Note that tea, coffee and alcohol are diuretics which means they cause the body to lose water, so you may have to increase your water intake if you drink much of these.

STIMULANTS

Like the rest of the population, many artists are attracted to caffeine. Caffeine is a stimulant that is found in coffee, tea, chocolate and cola drinks. Caffeine creates physiological effects that are similar to those of adrenalin. Excessive caffeine intake can lead to increased heart rate, breathing and anxiety. Artists are usually stimulated more than enough by a performance without needing the extra stimulation of caffeine, so it would be wise to reduce your caffeine intake leading up to and during a performance.

Nicotine in tobacco can also act as a stimulant and therefore is better avoided before and during performances. However, if you are a heavy smoker, it would be unwise to cut down your nicotine intake drastically before a performance because of the withdrawal symptoms this would probably create.

EATING BEFORE PERFORMING

It is important to think about the timing of your meals before your next performance. You don't want to be hungry before you perform, but nor do you want to have a heavy, undigested meal in the stomach. The nutritionist Rosemary Stanton in *Eating for Peak Performance* (1988) makes these recommendations about eating before an important event.

1. Eat two to three hours before the performance.
2. Drink plenty of fluid, preferably water.
3. Include complex carbohydrates in the meal such as cereals, wholemeal bread, muffins, rice, pasta, vegetables, especially potatoes or fruit.
4. Avoid foods high in proteins and fats, as these take longer to digest.
5. Eat foods that are familiar and enjoyable to you.
6. Avoid large quantities of sugary foods because these give uneven bursts of energy.

If you want to snack shortly before or during a performance, try eating fruit, especially bananas, bread or sandwiches, juices, low-fat milk or crispbread. If you have difficulty eating food before performing because of anxiety, eat a little, and as often as you can. Use the relaxation and other strategies outlined earlier to help reduce the nausea.

EATING BREAKFAST AND LATE-NIGHT SNACKS

Rosemary Stanton strongly recommends eating breakfast as a regular part of your day. The purpose of breakfast is to break the 'fast' after the night. In the morning your body's energy is low and when you miss breakfast, the body's energy level remains lower for the rest of the day than when you eat breakfast. If you don't normally eat breakfast try doing some activity before eating. Starting with fruit or fruit juice can be a good easy way to get yourself into the habit of having breakfast.

Often, artists like to eat after a performance at night because they haven't eaten much before the performance. Eat as lightly as you can late at night before going to sleep: eating heavily will interfere with your sleep pattern as the digestive system actually slows down at night.

EATING ON TOUR

Another important aspect is what to eat when you are away from home. When you are on tour, you are at the mercy of the food that is available where you are. There is a temptation to eat convenience foods more than usual and to eat at irregular times. For all the reasons outlined above, it is just as important to follow your normal diet whenever possible. This can be difficult on tour, because of the travelling involved and because foods may be unfamiliar when in a foreign country, or familiar foods may be unavailable.

When you are arranging accommodation for your tour, have your manager, or organiser, find out what types of food are available where you will be staying. You might even want to change where you stay according to the food available. As much as possible, try to eat at your normal routine times and attempt to eat mostly from the complex carbohydrate group. You may like to take some food with you, if it is the type of food that you think will be hard to get where you are going. This could include your usual breakfast cereal, dried fruits or snack bars.

DRUGS

When you are feeling under stress or depressed, there is more of a temptation to use drugs, such as caffeine, nicotine, alcohol, marijuana and many others. Caffeine and nicotine are dealt with above. Alcohol is a sedative that artists sometimes use to relax and reduce tension. It does have a short-term relaxing effect and recent medical research even indicates that it can have health benefits; for example, red wine with a meal is thought to reduce cholesterol levels and aid digestion.

However, drinking to reduce tension before a performance can have some disadvantages because it reduces mental sharpness and physical reaction time. Alcohol can also disturb normal sleep patterns. A jazz musician told me of a musician he once played with in a band who had too much to drink. The intoxicated musician thought he was sounding great on stage, but the rest of the band members had to work hard to cover for him because his timing was out. Using alcohol to calm the nerves can also lead to a dependency on it before performing, so that after a while, you can't perform without it.

Some artists like to smoke marijuana before performing as they feel this helps them become more mellow. Once again, this is a two-edged sword because there is evidence that regular marijuana use reduces mental sharpness and motivation. In spite of all these cautions, though, most substances with the exception of nicotine, are fine if taken in moderation.

One group of drugs that is prescribed by doctors for performing artists is beta blockers. Beta blockers help reduce the physical symptoms of performance anxiety by slowing down the heart rate. They do not act directly on mental processes, but because they can make the artist feel physically calmer, they can help him feel mentally more at ease as well. Some artists do not like beta blockers because they tend to flatten the emotions and the artists don't feel as involved in the performance as they would like. If you would rather perform without the aid of drugs, you can use the mental techniques outlined in this book instead of taking beta blockers. If you do want to try beta blockers, do it under the supervision of a doctor, because the timing of a dose before performing is critical to achieving the desired effect.

Vincent Furnier, who became famous as the rock star Alice Cooper, described how he struggled to maintain the expectations of his performance persona:

> I had to drink two bottles of whisky a night just to cope with Alice. I say cope, because I felt I had to be Alice all the time, otherwise the audience would lose their love affair with Alice. What I didn't realise was that you can't live an intense character like that all the time, that's what happened to Jim Morrison and Keith Moon.
>
> *Quoted in Fowles, 1992.*

EXERCISE

Exercise can be a great method for reducing the tension and anxiety associated with performing. As well, it helps to increase physical energy levels and sharpen mental abilities. Without exercise or physical activity, people become increasingly tense, unfit and lacking in physical energy. Exercise increases the body's ability to ward off disease and become more resilient. Aerobic exercise, such as brisk walking, jogging or swimming, is especially good at cleansing the body of the build-up of stress-related chemicals.

WHAT'S THE BEST EXERCISE FOR ME?

The three main types of exercise are aerobic, anaerobic and stretching. Aerobic exercise works on using the major muscle groups of the body, increasing heart rate and oxygen intake. Some common types of aerobic exercise include jogging, aerobic classes, brisk walking, cycling, swimming and social dancing. Aerobic exercise helps to directly counteract the effects of the fight or flight response discussed in Chapter 1. To get the most value out aerobic exercise, it is necessary to exercise at least three times per week for a minimum of 30 minutes each time. The aerobic effect on the body does not 'kick in' until after about 15 minutes of exercise. To carry out aerobic exercise effectively, aim for a level where you are slightly puffing and you can feel your heart pounding. Artists, such as dancers, who engage in very physical activity can gain a significant advantage by doing aerobic exercise, because they are often not very fit aerobically, despite being anaerobically fit.

Anaerobic exercise works on increasing your muscle strength and tone. Some common types of anaerobic exercise are weight lifting, circuit-training classes, chopping wood and heavy gardening. Anaerobic fitness will be more or less important depending on the type of performing you do. Anaerobic fitness would be vital for a dancer but much less so for a stand-up comedian.

Stretching exercises help to produce flexibility in the major muscle groups. They also help to prevent injury when done before and after aerobic exercise by increasing blood flow to muscles. Some common types of stretching exercises include back stretches, toe-touching and yoga postures. Most artists need to include some stretching in their pre-performance warm-up, particularly of the muscle groups that will be used in the performance.

A good exercise program will include a combination of all these different types of exercise, although for general stress reduction regular aerobic exercise is the best.

Whether you engage in structured exercise activities or not, you can improve your physical condition in small ways by doing such things as taking the stairs instead of the lift, walking short distances rather than driving, carrying your shopping bags instead of using the shopping trolley, or going for a walk during breaks. Find an exercise you enjoy doing so that you are motivated to do it regularly.

PHYSICAL INJURY

One way to sustain your performance levels at their peak is to prevent injury. The types of injury that occur in the different performing arts are now being better documented. For example, pianists are prone to suffer hand and wrist problems; dancers, spinal problems; and actors, miscellaneous ailments. As always, prevention is better than cure. There are several factors involved in prevention, including good posture, safe practice techniques and warming up and stretching before practice and performing. For example, it is valuable for a piano player to regularly do some stretching exercises in the hands, arms and shoulders before and after playing. Dancers need to include a cardiovascular component and stretching in their warm-up before dancing full out.

To help prevent overuse injury, it is advisable to take short breaks during practice sessions and stretch the muscles you are using frequently. General stretching exercises which involve the whole body will also help to increase blood circulation and flexibility. Posture and movement techniques such as the Alexander technique, Feldenkrais method and hatha yoga will help reduce injury as well as improve technical facility through better posture and movement.

It is well known that stress is connected with health problems. A research study of orchestral musicians found that those who regularly experienced high stress levels also experienced more health problems, including overuse injuries, than their colleagues who experienced lower stress levels. This finding suggests that managing your stress is one preventative way of reducing injury and ill health.

SLEEP AND REST

My research with professional musicians found that most of them like to nap or rest before a performance. Sleep helps refresh both the body and the mind. An important function of sleep is to enable you to mentally process the day's events, so that when you awake in the morning, you don't have the memories of the previous day on your mind and you feel like it is a *new* day. If you have disturbed sleep, you will experience irritability, difficulty in concentrating and feel less creative and more worn out.

If you are having trouble sleeping, here are some suggestions that may help.

• Reduce caffeine intake before sleeping and instead have warm drinks that have a more sedative effect, such as hot milk, herbal teas or caffeine-free hot drinks.
• Maintain, as much as possible, a regular time for sleeping.
• Wind down half to one hour before sleeping and avoid mentally stimulating pursuits before going to bed.

- Avoid eating meals close to bedtime, and if you want a late-night snack eat complex carbohydrates such as bread.
- Good physical exercise during the day will tire the body and promote sleep.
- Reduce muscular tension with a hot bath, massage or relaxation tape.
- If you smoke, reduce the number of cigarettes you smoke as nicotine acts as a stimulant.
- If you are overweight, a reduction in weight will help you to sleep by reducing strain on the body.
- Keep your bedroom cool and quiet, and sleep on a comfortable firm mattress.

ACTIVITY 1: ASSESSMENT OF PHYSICAL FACTORS
Regularly assess how well you are doing in the areas of diet, exercise, sleep, practice habits and drugs. Are you close to your ideal in these areas or are there some changes you could make? Begin to notice how these physical factors affect your ability to practise, rehearse and perform.

7 Are You Achieving What You Set Out to Do?

> Our plans miscarry because they have no aim. When a man does not know what harbour he is making for, no wind is the right wind.
>
> *Marcus Annaeus Seneca*

When you are deciding to go on a holiday, your first consideration is usually based on what excites or interests you. There are lots of choices to tempt you, from a get-back-to-nature holiday, city-based, historical tour, travel to a foreign country, romantic get-away, family holiday or a 'peace-and-quiet' holiday.

If you are *excited* about going on a holiday, it is easier to save the money required for it, to make the necessary plans, arrange for transport and accommodation, overcome obstacles and stay focussed on doing what you need to do to make it happen. Someone who really wants to go on a holiday demonstrates her desire by her commitment to achieving her goal. Striving for goals in performing is similar in principle to going on holiday. It requires a passion for performing and a commitment to undertake the necessary steps to achieve the goal.

INTRINSIC MOTIVATION

When you are motivated by a desire from within yourself, this is intrinsic motivation. If you are intrinsically motivated to perform, you gain fulfilment from performing in itself, even if this does not lead to any external rewards. Someone who pursues a hobby for example, is intrinsically motivated because he gains satisfaction from simply doing it, although he might also be motivated by external factors such as earning money or recognition from his hobby.

If as an artist you find that the process of performing is in itself fulfilling then you are intrinsically motivated. Sometimes, you will perform on occasions where it is required or expected of you, and sometimes you will perform in situations that you would prefer not to be in; for example, when the audience is uninterested or unappreciative of the performance.

Becoming a successful artist requires commitment. There needs to be something inside you that helps you bounce back if the going gets tough. I have found that most people who perform seriously, as opposed to those who do it as a casual interest, have a passion for performing which has often developed in childhood. The reason someone develops a passion at a young age for the performing arts, let alone anything else, is not well understood. Sir Robert Helpmann, the ballet dancer and actor, grew up on a sheep station in an isolated part of Australia where his exposure to the arts was minimal. When asked why he thought he became interested in dance, he said he had no idea why but he couldn't remember wanting to do anything else. His sister commented that he had always been the natural director in their childhood plays and even as a child he had shown a natural ability for moving beautifully.

As an artist, your passion for performing can become submerged by the associated demands of performing. Artists' early experiences of music, dance and acting are usually remembered with pleasure. But as artists develop their art and practise it at an advanced level, the underlying passion can be swamped by the discipline of training, having to forgo other opportunities for the sake of performing, and the disappointment of setbacks.

The prima ballerina Irina Baronova commented on the disadvantage of losing the intrinsic joy of performing. 'When I was dancing, we loved our art. There was the desire to work together with joy and with energy it was not work, it was not a job. I see dancers for whom this is a job and when it becomes a job, I'm afraid it doesn't come over the footlights and touch the audience's heart.' (The *Australian*, 20–21 August 1994.)

Passions can change, and just because you have pursued an interest or career in performing, for example, it does not mean you have to continue doing this. I know a person who had performed as a professional musician for 10 years for musical stage productions in his early adult life and then decided to sell real estate, which he did successfully.

Karin had studied ballet as a girl and given it away during her teens to pursue a successful career in another field altogether. After having a family and while still engaged in her professional career, she decided to return to dance as a mature-age student. She expressed her fulfilment from dance as something that made her feel whole and cleansed. She returned to doing ballet classes, and although she naturally felt out of place participating in classes with young girls, she was determined to present for an important dance exam which would then recognise her as a teacher of dance at a professional level. She achieved this goal, which proved to be a difficult but fulfilling one for her.

EXTRINSIC MOTIVATION

A person who is motivated to act because of factors outside of herself is said to be extrinsically motivated. Extrinsic factors could include financial reward, recognition and expectations from others, including the general public, teachers, parents, peers, approval from an artistic director or manager, or a record company. External goals that would reflect extrinsic motivation might be obtaining entry to a professional dance or theatre company, gaining a recording contract, playing in a prestigious performance hall or winning an important film role. Goals such as these can provide an enormous spur for the artist to strive for higher achievement.

Extrinsic factors can also become a source of pressure for the artist. Jessie was a young woman in a rock band that had become commercially successful. She found that as they became more successful, the band experienced greater demands from its record company, manager and fans to continue to write and record successful songs. Before this, when the band members had been unknown, they were able to write music how and when they liked, without any concern for what others wanted. This had allowed them to write purely from an intrinsically motivated source rather than an extrinsic one. For well-known performers, the expectations of others are an ongoing source of pressure that they need to learn to manage.

The first requirement for achievement in performing is to be intrinsically motivated and to feel a passion for your art form. The second requirement is to be extrinsically motivated by giving your passion direction.

GOALS — THE WAY AHEAD

The first thing in life to do is to do with purpose what one proposes to do.
Pablo Casals, cellist.

The plans you make today bring about what you will be doing tomorrow. If you set out to do nothing in particular, you'll find that's what you'll be doing tomorrow. If you set out to achieve a specific goal and commit yourself to achieving it — that is likely to be what you are doing tomorrow. Goals set direction and focus your thoughts and actions towards that direction.

To use our holiday example again, if you were to get into your car and go on a holiday without any idea of where you were going, you could end up anywhere, which might or might not be the type of place you'd like to spend your holiday. On the other hand, if you had chosen a destination for your holiday, you would know where you wanted to go and you would use a map to help you find your direction. You would also prepare for your holiday with the destination in mind, knowing what type of clothes, food and equipment you would need.

There is plenty of evidence in many fields of human endeavour to demonstrate that people who set goals, work on steps to achieve them and persist in working towards them, are the achievers in their fields of endeavour. As an artist wanting to realise your potential, the same applies to you.

THE DREAM GOAL

The first step in making goals is to set an overall 'dream' goal. This is a goal that you would dearly love to achieve, even if you're not sure of how you will achieve it, and even if you have some doubt about your ability to achieve it.

> Glen was a part-time professional opera singer whose dream goal was to become a freelance professional in Europe. As we worked on how to achieve his dream goal, he became clearer on what he needed to do to succeed. He realised he had avoided taking the necessary steps required. He began to make major life changes which would support him in achieving his goal. One of these changes included having less contact with his immediate family who he found was not supportive of his aspirations and, instead, spending more time with friends and professional associates who were supportive of him. This culminated in him leaving his home country and moving to Europe and starting life there with renewed optimism.

The most important feature of a dream goal is that it is something that you feel you can commit yourself to, and something that excites you when you imagine achieving it. There will be times when you feel self-doubt or defeated in your efforts to achieve your goal, and if it is not something that energises you, then you will give up easily. It's worth spending time on working out your dream goal, because it will be something that you will be working towards for a long time. It is also good to enjoy the process of achieving your goal, as this will help you stay motivated. Realise that the process of achieving your goal is a learning experience and it is this that enables you to grow as an artist.

There will be times when your commitment to your goal will be tested because it will seem that you are moving away from it rather than closer to it. If you have ever been walking in the hills, you may remember having the following experience. As you stood on top of the first hill and looked out across the valley before you, it seemed that the next hilltop was not too far away. However, once you had walked down into the valley between the hills, it seemed as though the second hill was further away than when you started. In reality, you are much closer to the goal than when you started, even though it does not *feel* like it. These perceptual illusions

> A friend of mine, a full-time housewife, could not read music and played her instrument out of time . She dearly wanted to be in a semi-professional folk band playing regular gigs. She worked and worked on her playing, and performed with as many other accomplished musicians as she could. A few years later, after having not seen her during this time, I saw her playing perfectly one night as the leader of her own band. Her achievement might have seemed only a small thing to the casual observer, but she had attained exactly the level of achievement she had wanted.

are just that, illusions, and they require you to retain a rational commitment to your goal to pass through them.

Your dream goal does not have to be a world-beating one. If you are an amateur artist, your goal might be to participate in a local repertory production. If you are a professional, your goal might be to play the lead role in a major film. Everyone sets their own level of achievement, and having reached this, they can then set higher goals, if they wish.

PRACTICAL GOALS

Having set your dream goal you must establish practical goals that will take you to your destination. These are the how-to goals that describe the steps you need to take to achieve your dream goal. These goals will be modified as you go along and will become clearer as you get closer to your dream goal. What is most important is that you set these as realistic achievable goals and take action towards reaching them. They can be seen as smaller steps along the way to achieving your dream goal. When you break down big goals into smaller steps, the task becomes far more manageable than just seeing the big goal. Working out the smaller steps will motivate you to take action.

Here are some suggested categories for breaking down your practical goals into different time frames:

- long-term (months to years)
- short-term (weeks to months)
- immediate (today)

Andrew was a student guitarist who was feeling overwhelmed by his performance schedule leading up to a major end-of-semester exam. He had three pieces to prepare for this exam and they were at different levels of readiness. One piece he had performed successfully before and felt he only needed to brush up on, the second piece he had done a lot of work on and was halfway ready, and the third piece, a difficult contemporary piece, he had only gone over a few times. He had about a month to go before the exam. His short-term goal was to have them all at a state of readiness to pass his exam. We worked out how many hours of practice he would need to put in for each piece, and when. We also worked out what in particular he needed to master in each piece. For the first piece, this involved playing through the piece to familiarise himself with it again. For the second piece, he needed to identify the difficult passages which required further work, while he could leave the easier passages alone till closer to the exam. For the third piece, he needed to go through it comprehensively, as he would when normally learning a piece. I also suggested that he do some mental rehearsal of this piece to bring his skill level up more quickly. His short-term goal of passing his exam was only one step towards achieving both his long-term goal of completing a degree in music performance and his dream goal of becoming a professional teacher and artist.

Here are some guidelines to help you set your goals:

1.   State them in the positive; that is say what you want to achieve not what you don't want. For example, in the case of the guitar student his short-term goal was to pass his exam, so he wouldn't state his goal as, 'I want to avoid failure'. He might state his goal as 'I want to pass my music exam; the grade isn't important as long as I pass', although he could state as his goal a higher grade if it was important to him.

2.   Be specific about your goal. This means that you will know precisely when you have achieved it. The more detail you can use to describe your goal, the better. Being precise usually means putting an exact date on when you want the goal achieved by. Goals that are stated imprecisely tend to lead to procrastination rather than action.

3.   Make goals, with the exception of your dream goal, that are realistically attainable. Setting unrealistic goals will lead to disappointment and a feeling of failure when you find you are consistently not achieving them. In the case of the guitar student, given the preparation time he had left for his exam, it was more realistic to aim for a pass rather than for a higher grade.

4.   Set goals that are a challenge to you. If all the goals you set are easy to achieve, you are not going to feel stretched and will not develop your talents.

5.   Write down your goals. Goals require action and the first step you can take is to write them down. This also helps to crystallise what it is you want to achieve and gives you a greater sense of commitment. It is always rewarding to look back over what you have written down some time later and see how much you have achieved.

6.   Develop images of yourself succeeding in your goals. Imagine what it will feel like when you achieve your goal, how others might react to your achievements and how it might change your life.

7.   Change your goals as you become clearer about what you want to achieve and as your ability grows. It is not always easy to be clear about your goals initially, but as you move towards them, you become clearer, even if that means finding out that a particular goal is not what you wanted after all. Developing new goals is important for professional artists who have achieved their initial aims and now need to create new challenges for themselves.

8.   Stay focussed on the goals and not on the obstacles to achieving them. It is very easy when obstacles come your way to let go of your goals or reduce your expectation of what you can achieve. When the going gets tough, ask yourself 'Is the goal something I really want to achieve?' If your answer is yes, stay focussed on the goal and you will eventually find a way around the obstacle. If the answer to your question is no, then it will be necessary to reconsider your goal. Before giving up a goal, be very careful you are not giving it up because the effort of striving for it is making you too uncomfortable.

9.   You may think that it is not until you achieve your goal that you will experience

a sense of fulfilment and enjoyment. In fact, it is the process of achieving your goals that is often very memorable and it is worth enjoying this process. Have you noticed, for example, that when you have gone to the top of a mountain to admire a wonderful view, the view seems much more satisfying if you have walked up to the top rather than if you have driven there by car?

PERFORMANCE GOALS

The essence of all art is having pleasure giving pleasure.

Mikhail Baryshnikov, dancer.

When I play, I make love, it is the same thing.

Artur Rubinstein, pianist.

Having discussed goals for general development, let's now focus on goals specific to performing. These goals arise from the question 'When I give a performance, what is it I am trying to achieve?'. Having worked with many artists on this question, I have concluded there are performance goals that are specific to a particular performance, and goals that apply to every performance.

Why bother with performance goals? I have been struck by the number of artists who, when asked what they are trying to achieve in a performance, have to stop and think about their answer, which suggests they're not always focussed on their goals for performing. Performance goals focus you in the present, before and during a particular performance. This helps you become task-relevant in your mental focus and emotionally engaged in your performance.

GENERAL PERFORMANCE GOALS

Among the common general performance goals artists have, are to inspire and move the audience, to achieve technical accuracy, to obtain personal enjoyment in the performance, to be true to the composer's or choreographer's or writer's wishes, to express one's intentions through the performance, to become lost in the performance, and to do one's best. Different artists place different levels of importance on each of these goals.

The English comedian and comedy writer, Ben Elton, commented on his performance goal when he said in a newspaper interview, '... the only way you can hope to please your audience is to please yourself. If you write dishonestly, trying to appeal to some amorphous idea of what your audience is or what's hip, then you will fail, not only as an artist but as a person.' Like Ben Elton, many artists believe that their first goal is to enjoy their own performance, and if this happens, their performance will reach a standard that will make it a better performance for the audience.

SPECIFIC PERFORMANCE GOALS

Specific performance goals are goals that apply to a particular performance or production; for example, wanting to achieve a particular mood or feel in a performance, wanting to overcome a certain technical problem, producing a good ensemble or group effect, choosing some songs, pieces or a play that you think will be enjoyable or challenging for a particular audience. Here is an example of how you might set specific goals for a performance.

Emma, a professional musician, explained to me that she had just given one of her worst performances for a long time. She had played in a lunchtime concert with an audience that contained many 'fidgety and talkative children' who were sitting in the front row. Where she was positioned, it was very hot because she was sitting in front of a huge glass window with direct sunlight streaming through. This made her feel physically uncomfortable and also made her cello go out of tune. After the concert, she asked one of her fellow musicians how she thought the concert went. Her colleague said she had enjoyed it. Her colleague also said she had played there before for a similar concert, and consequently, knew what conditions to expect. I suggested to Emma that she had had little control over the performance conditions on the day. For future performances at this venue, I suggested that she was better off accepting those aspects that she could not change and to change her specific performance goals to suit the occasion. She had a repeat performance coming up and decided that for this concert she would be more accepting of the performance conditions, set her musical goals more modestly, and enjoy the performance. She did this and was much happier with her performance, even though it wasn't a career highlight!

Of course, sometimes artists become confused about what they are trying to achieve in a performance. An extreme example of this was Nicol Williamson, who was appearing as Hamlet in Boston, before a limited run on Broadway. 'On opening night, he suddenly announced, in the middle of a scene, that he was giving up his acting career and walked offstage. After he calmed down somewhat, he returned to his performance amidst general applause.' (Hay, 1989.)

ACTIVITY 1: DREAM GOALS
Close your eyes, take a few deep breaths and relax. Imagine yourself doing just what you would like to be doing as an artist. Without censoring it in any way, write down those things you would truly like to be doing, these become the basis of your dream goals. These goals can change or become more refined as you become clearer about what you want to do. They determine your overall direction.

ACTIVITY 2: GOAL SETTING
Taking your dream goal, work backwards and determine what are the long-term, intermediate, and short-term goals you need to achieve to reach your dream goal. This exercise can take quite a while to do because you need to think and reflect on a number of aspects of your goal. You will not be sure of all the steps you need to take straight away, particularly the longer-term ones, but make the best guess you can. Setting

goals that are nearer to the present will be easier and you will feel motivated to achieve them because they are more immediate. Remember the saying attributed to Lao Tzu, 'The journey of a thousand miles begins with one step'. Each step you take in the right direction builds up your momentum. Goals are about motivating you to take your first step and making sure it is in the right direction.

ACTIVITY 3: PERFORMANCE GOALS
Write down what you are attempting to achieve in every performance you give. What do you hope to gain from your performance for yourself, for your fellow artists and for the audience (general performance gaols)? What are the specific things you want to achieve in your next performance (specific performance goals)?

8 Developing Your Performance Routine

We first make our habits, and then our habits make us.
John Dryden

WHAT IS A PRE-PERFORMANCE ROUTINE?

Have you ever thought about what is the best way to prepare yourself for a performance? You may have noticed that some artists seem to have it all together before a performance, while for others, it is a hit-and-miss affair. To consistently deliver a good performance, you need to follow a well-developed way of preparing *yourself* for performing. As the quote above suggests, developing a routine that works for you will be well worth it.

There are often factors outside of your control that can potentially interfere with performing. The best way to deal with these factors is to minimise their influence as much as you can and to maintain your inner control. The pre-performance routine is a way of ensuring that your inner control is reliably maintained no matter what the outside conditions. This routine brings together all the aspects discussed in previous chapters as an integrated pattern for performance preparation.

A reliable pre-performance routine will help you to feel secure as you approach a performance and this will lessen your chances of experiencing overwhelming anxiety. Ultimately, you need to develop a routine that works for *you*. Your routine may also vary to some extent according to the type of performance you are preparing for.

To develop a pre-performance routine, you need to consider each of the following four areas: artistic, psychological, physical and organisational. Considering each of these elements in performance preparation will lead to your routine being more refined. In the outline below the four different areas are divided into long-term and short-term strategies. Long term means the weeks and months before a particular performance, which is most of the time. Short term means the few days before a performance, up to and including the last moment before going on stage. For convenience, I have designed the pre-performance routine as though you were preparing for one major performance. In reality, most artists are preparing for several performances at the same time. Bearing this in mind, adapt all the four elements to fit into your schedule.

ARTISTIC PREPARATION

LONG-TERM STRATEGY

For long-term preparation, the most crucial aspect of your artistic preparation is to be continually developing your skill in your performance area so that you are constantly improving at a technical level. This requires regular practice and learning from teachers and fellow artists. Listening to and observing others will also improve your skills. Research has shown that simply observing someone who is very skilled at an activity teaches our subconscious mind how to improve in that area of skill.

Developing your interpretation of your character, piece or song for a performance requires a process of exploration and thought. This might, for example, incorporate reading about a composer's ideas on the work or learning about the culture in which a play is set. For example, Dustin Hoffman spent considerable time investigating the medical condition of autism when preparing for his character in the film *Rainman* in which he plays an autistic adult.

A valuable and ongoing part of your long-term artistic preparation is to obtain objective feedback about your performance skills. One useful way of doing this is to record your performances, rehearsals and practice sessions. You will often be surprised at what you notice from recordings that you don't notice while you are actually performing.

It is very helpful to have some trial runs through the performance before the real thing. This can be done in two ways. The first is to simulate your performance by running through it by yourself, without stopping, while imagining there is an audience present. This is similar in principle to an airline pilot who trains in a simulated aircraft cockpit which never leaves the ground. The second way is to arrange for some preliminary performances, or previews, by inviting friends, family and fellow artists to attend your performance, thereby gaining feedback from your 'audience' afterwards. You might want to schedule one of your preliminary performances for the same time of day that you will actually be giving your real performance. If your performance is at a different time of day to when you would normally practise, it will feel less familiar to you when you do perform. Dress rehearsals also serve a similar function.

Other ways of arranging preliminary performances include performing without payment for community groups, such as church groups, retirement homes, youth groups, schools and charity groups. You will find that you can perform for these groups without feeling the pressure to produce your absolute best performance.

For professional artists, it is often good to have performance opportunities to air new material before presenting it in a real performance. The more often you are able to perform as part of your preparation, the more secure you will feel on the day. The more feedback you gain about your progress in performance conditions, the more confident you will become that your performance is secure.

SHORT-TERM STRATEGY

The main short-term strategy is to taper off your practice schedule as the performance approaches so as to keep your energy levels high and to prevent emotional staleness. Some anxious artists continue to practise and rehearse intensely right up to the performance, but this tends to reinforce a sense of panic and creates physical tiredness. The ideal situation is to know your material well before the performance date, so that in the last few days before a performance, you only need to engage in light practice. During the last few days you may only want to go over particularly difficult sections, rather than the whole performance.

PSYCHOLOGICAL PREPARATION

LONG-TERM STRATEGY

The fundamental aspect of your psychological preparation is to focus on the personal challenge of the performance. As we discussed in Chapter 2, there are definite benefits in perceiving your performance as a challenge, rather than as a threat. Follow the suggestions in Chapter 7 for establishing career goals so that a particular performance is seen as part of the overall development of your career. Part of your long-term preparation is to work out your goals for the specific performance you are working on, so that in practice and rehearsals, you are performing with these goals in mind.

As we discussed in Chapter 5, mental rehearsal can form a part of your long-term preparation. You can use this to improve skills as an adjunct to physical practice and rehearsal. You can also develop mental imagery for aspects of your performance to aid you in your emotional interpretation, such as the dancer thinking of a particular flower. Long-term practice with these images will allow you to call them up quickly during your simulated and preliminary performances. Closer to the performance, you can use mental rehearsal to build self-confidence and manage anxiety. To do this, imagine yourself in a relaxed state, completing your performance in the ideal way you want it to go.

Practising focussed attention (see Chapter 4) is part of your long-term preparation. This is an ongoing skill you can develop. Part of your preparation for a specific performance is to develop the ability to put mistakes in the past and stay focussed on the present. If you always practise this, it will come more easily in performance.

A most important form of psychological preparation is to use positive, realistic self-talk. During your long-term preparation, focus mainly on the types of self-talk listed under the 'Preparation' stage in Chapter 2. Remember the four sub-personalties and make sure you have worked out how to respond to the negative self-talk they produce.

SHORT-TERM STRATEGY

The short-term strategy as you come closer to the performance is to shift your self-talk to the 'Before' stage. Once again, how much you practise changing your negative self-talk to positive self-talk will determine how easily you are able to change it before and during your final performance, when it really counts. Negative self-talk tends to become more frequent the closer an artist comes to a performance, so set yourself up with positive self-talk well before this. Before you perform at any time, practise the centering exercise (see Activity 2 in this chapter) as a way of getting into the right mental and physical state. Closer to the performance, and certainly during it, engage in task-relevant thinking.

PHYSICAL PREPARATION

LONG-TERM STRATEGY

Long-term physical preparation for performance includes regular aerobic exercise, good nutrition and a lifestyle that promotes health and well-being, as outlined in Chapter 6. There is no benefit in performing with an injury, so your long-term preparation also involves good practice habits, incorporating warm-ups, stretching and breaks.

It is very valuable to include some type of relaxation as part of your preparation, because a stressed artist is not likely to perform very well. Furthermore, stressed-out habits can become part of the performer's normal daily routine and then he doesn't realise the level of stress he is under. Closer to the performance, it is certainly worthwhile using relaxation techniques more regularly because of the natural build-up in the autonomic nervous system which can lead to excessive anxiety if not kept in check.

Before a performance, it is valuable to obtain extra sleep and rest either by going to bed early the night before the performance, sleeping in, or taking a nap on the day of the performance. Even if you remain awake during the nap time and think calming thoughts or images, you will still gain some benefit. Avoid an excessive intake of caffeine and sugary foods close to the performance, and eat foods mainly from the complex carbohydrate group (see Chapter 6).

ORGANISATIONAL PREPARATION

LONG-TERM STRATEGY

Whether you are a professional or an amateur artist, work towards developing a lifestyle that supports your performing and your career goals. Develop relationships with people who support you in various ways, such as teachers, fellow artists, managers, professionals (for example, physiotherapists, voice specialists, psychologists), family and friends. Remember that no one person will provide all the support you need. Organising your time so that you meet your priorities, including non-performance demands, is essential to an effective performance career. Chapter 10 outlines some time-management strategies you can use.

Short-term Strategy

Closer to the performance, organise a trip to the performance venue, if possible. You may be able to observe other artists performing there and possibly organise a short practice there yourself. Your need to do this will vary according to your level of experience and the importance of the occasion.

Arrange for the day of your performance to be as 'hassle free' as possible, so you are not feeling worn out even before you begin the performance. Have your arrangements for transport, clothes, props, instruments and equipment worked out in advance. Arrive early for your performance — there is nothing more likely to make you tense and anxious than struggling through traffic thinking you are going to be late. Before going on stage, most artists find it helpful to be alone for a while to become mentally focussed on their performance. The time required for this will vary from a few minutes to an hour, depending on the individual. For artists who perform as part of a group, such as actors in a play, developing mental focus can be a group activity.

Placido Domingo, the opera singer, describes his pre-performance routine:

> I try to do minimal talking the day before. I sleep to about eleven-thirty, then I have a shower and breakfast. I cannot start the day if I do not have a shower ... especially the day of singing. After that I do my first trying [vocally] ... ten minutes. Then I like to walk, because that wakes me up. I go to the theatre where I am going to sing and maybe I try my voice again ... only five minutes, to have that feeling. Then I have a very light lunch at about two: consomme, steak, and coffee. Then I walk more and have a little nap for an hour, or an hour and a half. Then I take another shower about five-thirty, I walk to the theatre, and I do a couple of scales. I sing some of the phrases that I have in the performance ... some of the difficult stuff I want to try out ... before I go on stage.
>
> *Quoted in Hines, 1994.*

In summary, the different areas of your pre-performance routine can be divided up as follows:

Artistic Preparation

Long-term strategy
- practice and rehearse
- listen to and observe others
- develop artistic interpretation

Short-term strategy
- taper off practice
- keep 'your hand in'
- go over difficult parts

- simulate performance
- do preliminary performances
- record performances
- gain feedback from others

PSYCHOLOGICAL PREPARATION

LONG-TERM STRATEGY
- view performance as a challenge
- mentally rehearse the performance
- use positive self-talk for 'Preparation'
- develop mental focus

SHORT-TERM STRATEGY
- use positive self-talk for 'Before'
- focus on performance goals
- use task-relevant thinking
- mentally rehearse the performance
- 'centre' yourself before going on

PHYSICAL PREPARATION

LONG-TERM STRATEGY
- take regular exercise
- maintain good health
- remain injury free
- relax

SHORT-TERM STRATEGY
- increase relaxation practices
- practise breathing awareness
- do stretching exercises
- warm-up before performing
- take a nap/sleep/rest
- eat complex carbohydrates and minimise caffeine and sugars.

ORGANISATIONAL PREPARATION

LONG-TERM STRATEGY
- develop lifestyle around career goals
- develop plan for each performance
- cultivate support from others
- good time management
- familiarise yourself with venues

SHORT-TERM STRATEGY
- organise 'hassle free' day
- arrange transport, clothes etc.
- arrive early
- have time alone before performing

AFTER THE PERFORMANCE

On stage, I make love to 25,000 different people, then I go home alone.

Janis Joplin, singer.

So far, we have looked at how to manage the pre-performance routine. However, even for artists who give a very successful performance, the post-performance period can pose some problems. I have identified three phases in the post-performance recovery period.

The first phase is the period immediately following the performance, that is, as soon as the artist walks off the stage. If the performance has gone well, the artist usually experiences a natural high, a result of chemicals called endorphins which are produced in the brain. Compared with the period of introspection before the performance, this phase is often a time when the artist likes to be around other people, perhaps just to talk with other artists about how the performance went or to socialise with friends or family. If the performance has not gone well, the artist is more likely to want to be left alone and to be preoccupied with her own thoughts. If this is the case, it is good to recognise that this is not the best time to go into a deep analysis of the performance, because your view of it so soon afterwards is not a very objective one. At this time, the artist is still too aroused mentally and physically to be able to think objectively.

The second phase is the winding-down period when the body's neurochemistry is returning to normal after the heightened phase of the performance. At this time, the mind is usually very active: going over the performance or being engaged in other thoughts related to it. It is necessary for the mind and body to wind down before going to sleep and, for this reason, it helps if the artist does things that induce drowsiness (refer to Chapter 6 for some tips on how to encourage sleep). One professional musician told me he likes to listen to talk-back radio on his drive home. He definitely doesn't want to listen to music.

The third phase of recovery is usually the period one to two days afterwards, when the body's chemistry has now reacted the opposite way and the artist can feel physically let down. Emotionally, the artist may feel flat or even depressed, or as if something is missing. This emotional response is due to the body's chemistry still stabilising and partly due to the artist feeling there is less attention on him and less excitement now the performance is over. During a performance the artist is the focus of attention. After the performance the artist usually returns to the humdrum lifestyle of practice, rehearsals and so on, which can feel like a let-down. During this phase, it is good to do some activities you find enjoyable, things you don't normally do while the pressure is on before a performance.

An awareness of these natural phases in your recovery after a performance will help you to move through them more smoothly. The length and intensity of the phases will vary from one artist to the next, depending on their experience, how frequently they perform and other lifestyle factors.

ACTIVITY 1: PRE-PERFORMANCE ROUTINE
Go through the four areas of preparation, artistic, psychological, physical and organisational, and note what you currently do in each of these areas to prepare for a performance. Decide whether you are doing sufficient in each of these areas to be well prepared for performing. If you are not, start to experiment with those activities that you are leaving out, and if you feel you are doing enough, congratulations!

Activity 2: The Centering Exercise

This exercise is very helpful for artists shortly before going on stage. The purpose of the exercise is to check if you are in the right mental and physical state before performing, and if you're not, to change your state quickly. The actor and comedian Billy Crystal says that before he goes on to do a live show, he makes sure his feet 'feel right' on the floor, he takes a deep breath, opens the fly of his trousers to pull the front of his shirt down flat and thinks of his first line of dialogue which is usually 'Good evening ladies and gentlemen'.

1. Stand with feet apart, arms hanging by your side and allow the body to move to its own pace. It is usually easier if you close your eyes throughout the exercise, although this is not essential.

2. Focus your attention on your breathing and begin by taking slow, deep breaths (as in the breath awareness exercise in Chapter 3). Feel the breath going right to the bottom of the lungs each time you breathe in. With each breath out, feel the muscles of the body letting go. Feel the shoulders dropping, the jaw muscles becoming loose, the neck relaxing and so on. Feel tension draining out of the body through the soles of the feet and into the ground.

3. Now begin to think about what you want to achieve in your performance, your performance goal. Think of a visual image or a keyword or phrase that describes the way you want to feel when you go on to perform. Feel the qualities of this keyword or image fill your body so that you become the word or image.

4. To prepare to bring your attention back outside of yourself, think of some positive self-talk (for example, 'I'm well prepared') that gets your mind into a positive focus.

5. Open your eyes and retain the feeling that you have gained from the centering exercise, as though you are a little distant from what is happening around you.

With practice, this exercise need only take two minutes, although it is good to spend more time in the relaxation phase if you have the opportunity.

9 The 'Flow' Performance

Optimal experience is something we make happen.
M. Csikszentmihalyi

If you have been performing for a number of years perhaps you can think back to a performance that really stands out as one you could not have imagined having gone any better, where you achieved everything you set out to achieve in the performance, or maybe even surpassed your expectations. You may have found yourself taking risks in the performance which came off. You may have done things which you hadn't rehearsed and which seemed to spring out of you spontaneously. Perhaps the whole performance wasn't like this but parts of it were.

There are many terms that have been used to label human experiences such as this, including 'peak experience', 'optimal experience', 'being in the zone', 'ideal' and 'perfect'. These terms all refer to the same type of exhilarating experience. The American psychologist Mihaly Csikszentmihalyi has spent many years studying people's peak experiences, which he calls 'flow' experiences. In his book, *Flow: The Psychology of Happiness* (1992), he documents 'flow' experiences from people working in ordinary occupations to those engaged in special interests, for example, mountain climbers and performing artists.

> A concert pianist told me how he had given an outdoor performance with an orchestra in the summer in a London park. He said that many of the conditions did not seem ideal for there to be an outstanding concert, because many of the orchestral players were returning from holidays and would have been out of practice. It was outdoors and there was a casualness in everyone's attitude, and yet he said, to his amazement, the performance was stunning and it was one of his best ever.

In my research, I asked professional musicians about their best performances. They described these performances with a sense of awe and mystery. It seemed as if this experience was the peak performance experience for them, an intrinsic reason for being an artist. Usually they did not know how they had achieved such performances. What puzzled them was that sometimes when all the conditions seemed right for such an experience to occur, it did not, and sometimes when the conditions did not seem optimal for the experience to occur, it did.

The following excerpts from interviews with well-known performers give a flavour of what the experience of the peak performance can be like:

> We all share the simultaneous experience of forgetting who we are at a rock concert, losing ourselves completely. When the music gets so good everybody for a second forgets completely who they are and where they are ... if you have experienced that enough times, it starts to become something that you strive for, because it is so sweet.
>
> *Pete Townshend, rock musician, Kohut and Kohut, 1994.*

> There is nothing I have to say or have to do. It's like a chef who improvises. He knows the result of certain combinations, but there are always new combinations... I have no idea of time ... I get to the point where I think I have just started, then they (off stage) tell me one hour, 50 minutes.
>
> *Victor Borge, pianist and entertainer,* The Australian, *11–12 February 1995.*

> ... as I went on to the stage, the house was not even full, I felt this thing. I felt for the first time the critics had approved, that the public had approved, and they had created a kind of grapevine, and that particular audience had felt impelled to see me. It was an overwhelming feeling, a head-reeling feeling, and it went straight to my head. I felt the feeling I'd never felt before, this complete confidence. I felt, if you like, what an actor must finally feel: I felt a little power of hypnotism; I felt that I had them.
>
> *Laurence Olivier, actor, Spoto, 1992.*

> ... the magical performances are when you reveal the truth, even if it's only twice in a night. That's a magic night, when suddenly the truth is revealed by the artist to the audience, not through talk, but through feeling, emotion, and coordination of movement and music.
>
> *Alexander Grant, dancer, Newman, 1992.*

Some of the professional musicians I interviewed related the following experiences:

> I become completely unaware of anyone else around me. Sometimes, it's one of those miraculous situations that you are transcended to another plane ... you know you can't put a finger wrong, you know that whatever you're going to do is going to be OK, and because of that, you can take risks and you can do things that you have thought of doing but haven't done because you've been afraid you couldn't do it.
>
> *Concert pianist.*

> On a really good night, I can almost listen to myself playing, on a really good night, there's like a fund of the subconscious that will take it over and it will work. It can be so easy that you can actually say, 'Gee, how about that!' ... 'Listen to that, how did I do that, did I just play that, gee that's nice.' I mean, those nights are like

needles in a haystack, but that's a really good night and you have those, and you think now I know how that feels, now I'll use that tomorrow, no you won't. It's a more ephemeral thing than most people realise. I do believe that the less happens up there, [pointing to his head] the better the music will be, because the subconscious has got all the information, it's all there, if you know the subject you shouldn't have to work on it when you deliver.

Jazz guitarist.

In the best performances, it seems like you have more confidence in the members of the group ... and it's a form of communication ... or opening up myself to communicate with everyone ... feeling the vibrations from every musician.

Jazz saxophonist.

When the sound is nice ... you get very, very high and ... everything seems to be happening. It's a lovely full package ... you don't need to think during the performance because ... when you open your mouth and it sounds right, you stop thinking ... and this is a good performance because you are actually creating as you go, because all the other ingredients are right so you can meet with them beautifully, but if one of the ingredients is not there, well, that makes a bad performance.

Singer.

... it's a feeling of control, too, control over the entire piece and the audience and you feel that you can't do anything wrong, it's that sort of feeling ... And yet, with the bad ones, it's not a case of feeling that you can't do anything right, I mean, it's not the exact opposite of that. You still feel as though bits and pieces of it are working very well ... but I don't have that feeling of being in control, and that's what's really important to me, I think, in a good performance.

Opera singer.

THE EXPERIENCE OF FLOW

Mihaly Csikszentmihalyi believes that the flow experience is a distinct human experience and one that is similar across many activities; for example, the quality of the flow experience that a mountain climber might experience is similar to the flow experience of an actor, even though the activities are very different. The experience of the flow state can be achieved even in ordinary pursuits such as reading a book or chopping wood, and a person may not be in the flow state all the time but may slip in and out of it. In studies around the world, Csikszentmihalyi and his researchers have found that people from very different cultures experience flow in similar ways.

THE ELEMENTS OF THE FLOW EXPERIENCE

Csikszentmihalyi has found that in whatever activity a person engages in, there are several elements that characterise the flow experience.

1.   The activity is one that you find challenging and you perceive you have the skills to accomplish it successfully, even though it might stretch you to the limit of

your abilities. The activity requires a degree of skill which has been learned.

2.   During the activity, there is a merging experience between you and the activity so that you lose the sense of yourself as being separate from the activity.

3.   The activity has a definite goal or purpose, so you know what it is you want to achieve and you know when you have achieved it.

4.   During the course of the activity, you gain feedback about how you are progressing so you are able to assess whether or not you are succeeding in achieving your goal.

5.   During the experience, there is a total concentration on the task, so you are not aware of other concerns. During the activity, your attention is narrow and focussed on the present, not thinking too far ahead and not dwelling on the past.

6.   You feel a sense of control during the experience but you are not actively trying to control it. You are aware you are taking risks but you don't fear the consequences of failure. Even though you feel in control during the experience, there is a sense that something greater than yourself is making it happen.

7.   You lose self-consciousness during the experience so that you could be described as being in an 'egoless' state. You do not become self-analytical. After the experience is over you feel you have achieved something great and, consequently, feel more self-confident.

8.   During the experience, your sense of time is altered so that what seems like minutes to you could be an hour in real time.

9.   The experience is so enjoyable in itself that the experience of flow becomes *intrinsically* rewarding, so that you want to engage in it again and again, which can make it addictive.

FLOW AND THE PERFORMING ARTS

Performing is particularly well set up to create the necessary conditions for flow. It provides a challenge, which cannot be met without the development of skill. A performance has a definite beginning and end, and it is clear to the artist where these points are. During the performance, the artist gains feedback from the audience, fellow artists and himself, although the type and amount of feedback differs according to the types of performance. Because of the creative and emotional nature of performing, the artist is encouraged to give himself up to his role or the music. The performance process can be so exacting that it requires the artist's attention to be narrowly focussed on the task (task-relevant) and not on aspects outside the performance (task-irrelevant). The presence of an audience during a performance heightens the sense of occasion for the artist and increases his mental and physical alertness, encouraging him to be very focussed. The reward for an artist in achieving a flow performance is great. There is the sense of having accomplished something worthwhile, as well as experiencing a tremendous high during and after the performance. An artist may experience flow for a whole performance, or go in and out of it during the performance.

INCREASING FLOW IN PERFORMANCE

Are there ways of increasing the likelihood of the flow experience? Sports psychologist Sue Jackson (1992 & 1995) has studied the factors which help or prevent the experience of flow in athletes. Not surprisingly, she found that athletes perform at their best when in a state of flow. She also found that the state of mind most likely to create the flow experience for athletes was what she called 'optimal arousal'.

How can you increase the likelihood of experiencing a flow performance?

- Enjoying your performing is paramount. If you are performing in a way in which you do not feel involved, it will be more difficult for you to experience flow.
- The primary state of mind to experience flow is that of 'optimal arousal'. If you are overly anxious before performing and you see the performance as a threat rather than as a challenge, then it will be helpful to use techniques such as relaxation and positive self-talk, to bring yourself back in control.
- Being aware of your performance goals and being focussed on them in a performance will improve your mental focus and concentration.
- Performances which do not challenge your skills so that you are not stretched at all, or performances which are beyond your skill level, will reduce your chances of experiencing flow.
- Being thoroughly prepared for a performance through physical and mental practice will mean that you do not need to be focussed on yourself during the performance and instead, you can be solely focussed on the holistic aspects of the performance.
- Factors which make you more aware of yourself during the performance, for example physical injury or illness, are likely to increase your level of concern for yourself and take your focus away from the performance.
- The attitude of the audience is outside the artist's control and this is a factor which can help or hamper the flow experience.

> You know it does depend a lot on the audience too, they can make a good performance. So you know usually if you go out and an audience just sort of sits there looking blankly at you, it's discouraging so I do say that the audience does have a great ... effect on performance.
>
> *Jazz musician.*

- Other factors which can make it harder for the artist to increase her chances of flow include conditions, such as lighting, acoustics, handling by the stage management, physical conditions and the attitude of the other artists.

To summarise, the factors that increase your chances of having a flow experience are:

- enjoying your area of performance
- state of 'optimal arousal'

- focus on performance goals
- match between challenge and skill
- thorough preparation
- good physical health
- favourable audience
- favourable performance conditions

THE AUDIENCE AND FLOW

A performance not only offers the artists the opportunity for a flow experience, it also offers this opportunity to the audience. Live performances offer more of a challenge to an audience than watching or listening to a recorded performance. The potential for the audience to experience flow during a live performance is increased because of the social nature of a live performance. People's reactions are often intensified when experienced in a group situation. Also, a subtle and powerful interaction occurs between an audience and the artist during a performance which cannot happen at a recorded performance. When the audience is mentally focussed on the performance, its chance of experiencing flow is increased, but if the audience is distracted, the chance of flow is decreased.

FOCUSSING ON THE 'BIG PICTURE'

Chapter 4 examined the three different levels of attention in a performance, attention on yourself, on the audience or on the performance process. Placing attention on the audience is not helpful as it leads to anxiety. Attention on yourself is not helpful if you are using negative self-talk, but it is helpful if you are using positive self-talk or relaxation to reduce tension. Fixing your attention on the process of performing, through the use of task-relevant thinking, is the most helpful focus to have during a performance.

There is a level of attention beyond this, one that will increase the likelihood of flow, and this is putting your attention on the 'big picture'. The 'big picture' does not put your attention on any one thing but on the whole performance. There is an effortless and dynamic transfer of attention between yourself, the audience, and the process, without your attention being fixed on any one area. There is a sense you are one part of the whole, of being a part of something greater than yourself. This can be experienced as a sense of 'letting go'.

Creating the flow experience for yourself is likely to be the most challenging mental skill you will learn in performing, and something that will take time and experience to develop. For these reasons it offers the greatest personal reward for the artist and for the audience that has the pleasure of experiencing such a performance. An artist who is in flow is giving a performance of personal excellence. Having an awareness of the factors that characterise flow, and working towards obtaining them in your performing, will optimise your likelihood of experiencing flow.

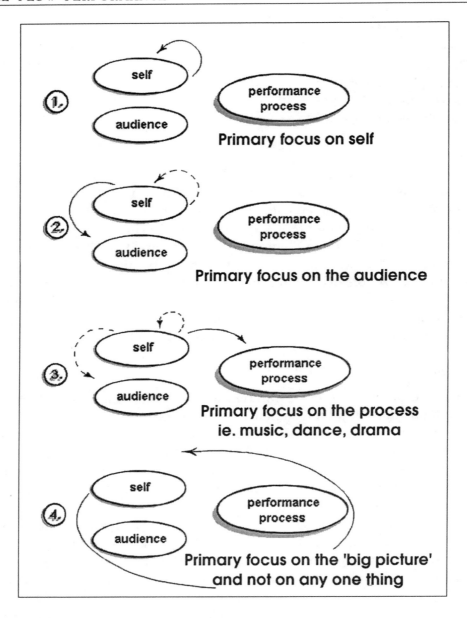

Keep in mind that the audience and other factors play a part in helping to produce the right conditions for flow, but if the external conditions are not ideal, do not let this prevent you from producing the conditions for flow within yourself.

ACTIVITY 1: CREATING FLOW IN PERFORMANCE
After examining the conditions required for flow, ask yourself how frequently you meet these conditions in your performing. Where you don't meet them, ask yourself what you can do to bring them about.

ACTIVITY 2: INTERNAL AND EXTERNAL FACTORS

Monitor your performances from now on and notice what internal and external conditions apply when you have a good or bad performance. It will help to keep a written record of this to refer to later. You will start noticing what helps you to perform well and what doesn't. You will also gain a better sense of what you can control and what you can't.

10 The Artist's Lifestyle

A musician must make music, an artist must paint, a poet must write, if he is to be ultimately at peace with himself.
Abraham Maslow

WHAT'S SPECIAL ABOUT AN ARTIST'S LIFESTYLE ?

Is there something special or different about being an artist? Artists are people first and artists second, and so are subject to lifestyle stresses in the same ways as everyone else. However, there are some characteristics that are special to the performing artist's lifestyle — particular stresses associated with performing. This chapter deals with issues that will have different relevance according to whether you are a professional or amateur artist.

Many areas of life are competitive, although the performing arts and the entertainment industry is one of the most competitive. There are more people who want to be successful professional artists than there are opportunities for them. Many a young person dreams of becoming a famous rock star, movie actor or well-known artist. As we saw in Chapter 7, to be successful it is necessary to have a dream of what you want to achieve. But it is often a long journey from creating the dream to fulfilling it. The path to a successful performance career can contain many hurdles, such as gaining admission to a training school or performance company, auditioning and being cast in a role, even before beginning to perform professionally.

The very nature of performance requires the artist to expose himself publicly, which usually leads to the experience of stage fright — something every artist needs to learn to manage. Being open to evaluation by an audience is something that does not occur in most other occupations. Artists can be faced with physical injuries arising from overwork, bad practice habits or simply accidents.

Financial worries are often a concern for professional artists as there is usually not a continuous and reliable source of employment in the performing arts. For this reason, artists often have to undertake jobs unrelated to performing — between roles, Marilyn Monroe worked in a wartime defence plant where she packed parachutes, and when she tired of this, she sprayed paint on target planes. (Fowles 1992, p50.) The gaps between work create anxiety for artists that is hard for the person in a nine-to-five occupation to appreciate. The actor Henry Fonda once remarked:

> If I have something down the line six months or a year away then I can handle myself. But if it is a period when I have no offers, I think, 'Well, that's it, Fonda. Nobody will ever ask you to work again.'

> *Fowles, 1992, p. 148.*

The performance lifestyle can create tension and anxiety because of the need for touring, late nights and unpredictable hours. I once interviewed a Russian concert pianist on tour and asked him what the weather was like back home, thinking he had just left his country. He said, 'I don't know, I haven't been there for three months'. This type of peripatetic lifestyle can place strains on the artist's family and social life.

Artists involved in long-running shows have special strains placed upon them. Peter consulted me after experiencing anxiety about damaging or losing his voice. At the time, he had a demanding role in a long-running and successful musical. Although medical tests did not reveal anything wrong with his voice, he found that upon waking in the morning, he felt the need to have 'a little sing' to make sure the voice was OK. He found that any slight change in vocal quality meant a day of torment for him and worry about how he was going to perform that night. After discussing the sources of anxiety with Peter, it became evident that he was experiencing burn-out. He confirmed that he still enjoyed performing and felt fully committed to his performance career. Also, the director and producer of the show continued to be supportive and gave him good feedback about his performances.

Because of the demanding role and the fact that it was such a long run, Peter was developing anxiety about stamina and vocal damage. He was becoming over-concerned about conserving his energy for the next performance. As a consequence, he was limiting his lifestyle by not going out, avoiding social contacts and not exercising. Outside of the show, he engaged in frequent negative self-talk, such as 'What if I lose my voice tonight?' and 'I'm a little tired, what if I miss the notes?'.

The solution for Peter was to change his negative self-talk and gradually increase his activities outside of singing to provide more balance and create a feeling of well-being. He also took up a daily exercise program, which increased his physical vitality. These changes made a world of difference for him and he started to enjoy life once more and lose much of his anxiety about his voice. Not long after he made these changes, he was able to take an extended break from the show, which gave him the opportunity for new work and alternative activities.

To the non-artist, the lifestyle of the artist can seem glamorous and exciting, and indeed, it can be. However, between the glamorous and exciting parts it is a daily slog. The general public attending performances for pleasure and relaxation, tends to see only the up side of performing, and not the years of determined effort that make artists successful at what they do. It can be hard for family, friends and acquaintances to fully understand the difficulties associated with the artist's lifestyle.

And Now for the Good News

There are many ways of dealing with the special stresses associated with performing. As we have seen, there are several techniques you can use in a systematic way to ensure that you manage stage fright, and that it doesn't manage you.

Refer to some of the preceding chapters which look at some of these techniques, such as mental attitude, relaxation, focussing of attention, positive self-talk and mental rehearsal.

The prevention of most physical injuries is under your control through using good practice habits, training with posture therapists or movement teachers, and understanding your physical limits.

The financial concerns need not be a major consideration for you. Most artists I have met are highly motivated individuals who can obtain other work that supports them during the down times. If you make sure all your financial obligations are being met, you will not be greatly stressed about this aspect. This is important, because when there is a build-up of stress outside of performance, it will flow over into your performing.

It is very valuable to have creative outlets other than in your performance area, so you can pursue them when you are going through quiet times and are not left feeling idle. You could also spend these quiet times improving your skills and knowledge of your field of performance. Having supportive people in your life who value you, whether or not you are working, can be very affirming. It is good to have friends and family who are not performing artists, as well as friends who share your profession. People outside of performing often have a more routine lifestyle, which can help you to 'keep your feet on the ground' and see things in perspective.

Criticism and Performing

Learning how to handle criticism is a necessary skill for all artists. During my research with professional musicians I found that they make distinctions between the different types of criticism they receive. They did not place much value on the appraisal of professional media critics, and saw these critics as not being well informed or useful from a technical point of view. Some even expressed a great dislike for media critics. But they accepted constructive criticism from fellow artists whose opinions they respected. They recognised that performing and watching a performance are subjective experiences, and two people attending the same performance can have different opinions on the same performance. For example, you might think you have given an excellent performance, yet the audience's response is lukewarm, and when you give a mediocre performance, the audience loves it.

I have found through my experiences that critics know what you're thinking or trying to portray as much as a baby in Afghanistan would understand when you speak English.

Dizzy Gillespie, jazz musician, Kimball et al, 1990.

I am sitting in the smallest room in the house. I have your review in front of me. Soon it will be behind me.

Max Reger, composer, Byrne, 1988.

A critic, after seeing a Martha Graham dance recital for the first time said he would not go back to see her: 'I'm so afraid she is going to give birth to a cube.' (Hay, 1989.)

In dealing with criticism, it is useful to assess the knowledge and the motives of the person it is coming from. Clearly, the critic commenting on Martha Graham's recital was not a fan of modern dance and his criticism probably had little to do with the quality of the performance. When you receive criticism, ask yourself: 'Is the person providing constructive criticism for my benefit? Is it another artist who is resentful of my success? Are they knowledgeable about my field of performance?' In others words, don't just accept criticism from anybody at face value. Artists with a self-critical personality are more likely to accept negative criticism from someone else as being a statement of truth.

At the other extreme, an artist who expresses an egoistic belief that everything he does is wonderful is likely to reject any criticism out of hand. He will turn the criticism back onto the person giving it, and conclude that it is that person who is biased. Such an artist is likely to miss out on the valuable insights that can be obtained from constructive criticism.

If someone gives you criticism and you judge this person's motive for doing so to be genuine, then the best way to respond is to listen to it, and thank the person for it! Immediately after a performance is not the best time to carry out detailed analysis of a performance, because you are in an emotionally sensitive state and are not likely to be thinking rationally. Allow one or two days after the performance to elapse before you do your post-mortem.

BUILDING TEAM SPIRIT

While artists often demonstrate a great deal of determination towards achieving their own performance goals, they do not always show such determination towards achieving harmonious relationships with those people around them. Being very single minded can lead to an intolerance of others, who seem to get in the way or don't behave the way some artists would like them to.

Many artists find themselves part of a performance group who is working to achieve a common goal. However, such groups do not always work harmoniously together and interpersonal conflict can result. Sports psychologist Terry Orlick (1990) has found the following three steps helpful in resolving conflict within sporting groups, and they are equally applicable to performing groups:

1.   It is valuable for the group to discuss and decide on its common performance goal so that everyone is working towards the same end.

2.   It is valuable for members of the group to express their individual goals so that personal agendas are out in the open and understood by the other artists.

3.   It is valuable for everyone to be committed to improving interpersonal relationships and making an effort to get along with others.

Here are some suggestions for getting on better with fellow artists:

- make the decision to get along
- get to know fellow artists
- avoid put-downs
- encourage each other
- take responsibility for your actions
- accept individual differences
- include everyone
- show others you care

It is useful to have regular reviews of progress in interpersonal relationships so any frustrations that may arise can be dissipated along the way and not be allowed to build up too much.

In many group performances, there is usually one person who makes the leadership decisions. In such cases, this person has a big influence in facilitating teamwork amongst individual artists. One important way for the group leader to do this is by keeping everyone's primary focus on the performance goal. Leaders can also inspire through their passion and skill. A member of a professional orchestra told me that one of his orchestra's best-ever performances occurred when the famous maestro Charles Dutoit conducted them for a major performance. What is interesting about this is that the orchestra was made up of the same players before and after the guest appearance of Charles Dutoit, so it was the team effect which he created which led to the superior performance.

A research study of classical string quartets confirmed what most artists experience. The study found that the quartets who were most successful professionally contained players who felt a genuine friendship for each other, and those that were least successful exhibited a lot of interpersonal conflict. Whether you perform in a small or a large performance group, your success will be partly determined by the quality of the interpersonal relationships within your group. Groups which contain a high degree of interpersonal conflict can be successful for a while, but eventually the growing tension will cause them to fall apart. The more focussed the artists in a group are on producing an inspired performance, the more personal conflicts will evaporate.

TIME MANAGEMENT

Chapter 8 discussed the value of the pre-performance routine and how this involves a combination of artistic, psychological, physical and organisational aspects. Integrating these aspects requires effective management of your time.

No one ever has enough time for everything, so the first principle in time management is to decide your priorities. These can include not only career or performance priorities, but also family, social, physical, financial, spiritual and other priorities. For good mental and physical health, it is important to balance all these aspects in your life so that no particular one dominates everything else.

Once you have established your priorities in these areas, the next step is to allocate the time required to achieve them. For example, if you included regular exercise as a priority, you might want to allocate three hours per week for this. You then work out the times of the week you would like to carry it out; for example, it might be a walk six times a week for half an hour in the morning.

After planning your week in this way, the third step is to plan the way you want your day to work out. This planning session might take five to ten minutes and can be done the night before or in the morning before you start your activities. Let's say you are planning your activities for today. Begin by making a list of the things you want to complete. Now divide them into one of the following three categories:

A   Priorities: things that need to be done today. As much as possible, do these things first, before any of the others.
B   Priorities: things that will need to be done at some time, but it is not absolutely necessary that they be done today. If you have time after your A priorities, this is when you do them.
C   Priorities: things you would like to do but they are not essential and it won't matter if they are never done. If you have time after all your A and B priority items, then you will do them.

B items that are not done today you can carry over to the next day, by which time they may have become A items. If, as you work through the day, it becomes clear that an A or B item is no longer necessary, then you can delete that item. Sometimes, as you work through your A items, you might encounter one that you don't like doing. It is part of developing good personal discipline that you do that item and not put it off because it is unpleasant.

If you follow this system you will find that *you* manage time rather than *time* managing you. You can write out your daily 'to do list' on a piece of paper each day or use a diary that allows enough space for you to fill in the details.

One other aspect of time management that can make a difference to your effectiveness is to distinguish between activities that are urgent but not important, and ones that are important but not urgent. You determine what is important according to the goals you have set. For example, daily practice is *important* to your goal of being a successful artist but it may not be an *urgent* activity, because there are no immediate consequences if you miss a day or two. If someone demands your time for something that doesn't have to be done that day but that person is simply impatient to have it done, it is easy to respond to her sense of urgency and perhaps miss out on your daily practice. It is urgent but not important. Remember, though, that daily practice is essential to achieving your performance goal and this person's demands could be dealt with after your practice. If you lead a full life, there will always be competing claims on your time, and you need to choose between those competing claims on the basis on what is important to your goals.

MISTAKES AS OPPORTUNITIES TO DEVELOP

It is never enjoyable to make a mistake, but the path leading to any successful human endeavour is littered with mistakes committed along the way. Artists who have succeeded have not done so overnight, and they have usually experienced many mishaps on the way. Artists tend to take 'failures' very personally because of the emotional investment they put into performing. It is more productive to treat 'failures' as opportunities to find out how you can improve your performing so you will be wiser and more skilful the next time around. As Samuel Smiles said: 'We learn wisdom from failure much more than from success; we often discover what will do, by finding out what will not do; and probably he who never made a mistake never made a discovery.'

When things do not seem to be going right for you, it is tempting to compare yourself with others who seem to be succeeding and to feel inadequate in comparison with them. Such comparisons are not helpful unless you gain an insight into yourself that will help you to develop. It can be inspiring to look up to others who have succeeded in a way you would like to, but constantly comparing yourself with your peers usually creates negative feelings and takes your focus off *your* goals. Accept that you are different from everyone else and your success is not going to be exactly the same as it is for others. It is your individuality that will distinguish you from others and help you to be noticed. Comparing yourself with others you admire is not the same, of course, as imagining yourself as an artist you aspire to emulate. As we saw in Chapter 5, this kind of positive mental imagery is very useful in overcoming performance anxiety.

If you are going through a difficult period, try this exercise. Imagine it is not you that is going through the bad period but a good friend. Imagine that this friend came to you for your help — how would you advise him, talk to him, support him? After answering these questions, apply your answers to yourself. Trust your opinion as you would that of a good friend.

BELIEF AND COMMITMENT

Your level of success in performing is likely to be largely determined by your belief in your ability and your commitment to achieving what you set out to do. Both these factors directly affect your level of motivation. Commitment comes from finding what you are doing is meaningful. If you are performing in areas or ways that do not inspire you it will be hard to maintain a commitment to your performing. Your commitment will increase if you are performing with a love for what you are doing.

Belief in your ability is an inner confidence that you can succeed in your chosen area. It is a belief in your potential. You may aspire to play in a role that you don't have the necessary skills for, but if you believe that with practice and experience you will eventually be able to play this role, then you are displaying good self-belief. It is extremely valuable to have others around you who also have belief in your abilities. If you doubt your abilities, take on small performance challenges and build up a record of success. This will then give you the confidence to tackle greater performance challenges. 'I believe anyone can conquer fear by doing the things he fears to do, provided he keeps doing them until he gets a record of successful experiences behind him.' (Eleanor Roosevelt, quoted in Buchan, 1991.)

What if your performance career does not turn out the way you wanted it to? Answer the question 'What would my life be like if I didn't become a performing artist?'. David Burns says in his book *Feeling Good* (1980) that 'A silent assumption that leads to anxiety and depression is "My worth as a human being is proportional to what I have achieved in my life".' As mentioned earlier, a healthy attitude to life as an artist requires a balance between performing and many other pursuits, including social, family, spiritual, physical and mental activities. If you see yourself as simply being a success or failure depending on how well your performance career goes, you are leaving out many other important aspects of your life in which success is also important. Life is bigger than just performing and your understanding of this will give you a sense of self-acceptance that goes beyond performing, and, paradoxically, a greater sense of freedom in your performing.

CONCLUSION

This book has covered skills for improving confidence as a performing artist. The first chapter looked at how artists create anxiety for themselves through perceiving performing as a threat. The following chapters looked at how performance anxiety can be managed through the use of breathing and relaxation, positive self-talk, task-relevant attention and mental rehearsal. The next chapter looked at how performance skills and confidence can be developed through the use of mental imagery. Chapter 6 discussed the effects of physical health on performance and how aspects such as diet and exercise can improve performance. Chapter 7 discussed how to increase motivation through goal setting and how this can be applied to individual performances as well as to the overall career of the artist. Chapter 8 explained the value of developing a pre-performance routine and how this helps the artist to produce consistently excellent performances. Chapter 9 described artists' experiences of the flow performance and what factors are more likely to make this state achievable. This final chapter has highlighted some of the special features of an artist's lifestyle.

In using any of the mental skills covered in this book, be prepared to experiment and allow time to implement them. These skills are like any other skill — they require practice to develop and to incorporate into your physical, technical and artistic preparation for performing. Carol Easton (1991), in her biography of the cellist Jacqueline du Pré, gave an indication of how one of the world's great performers viewed the performance process in this quote: 'Walking on stage — the recognition, the applause, the rumble of interest from the audience when I appeared. It never occurred to me to be nervous. I thought of the audience as a group of friends who had come to hear me play, and I found that very moving. I just *played*, and enjoyed it. Thinking about the notes would have spoiled the enjoyment. The work was all done beforehand.'

History reveals that the human race has a long tradition of the performing arts, with people engaging in some form of music, dance and drama. Present day society also offers a great deal of recognition to the performing artist. It is a very special experience for an artist to experience the thrill of moving an audience by an uplifting performance. For this reason, whatever your contribution is to the performing arts, you have a privileged and exciting role to play.

APPENDIX
Scripts for
Relaxation Tape

PROGRESSIVE MUSCLE RELAXATION

Now take up a position lying down ... or sitting back in a comfortable chair. Uncross arms and legs ... loosen any tight clothing ... and close your eyes. You are about to carry out a simple awareness exercise which will involve you becoming aware of various sensations in your body.

First bring your attention to your left arm, and your left hand in particular. Clench your left hand into a fist. Clench it tightly and study the tension in your hand and forearm. Focus on that tension and now ... let go. Relax the left hand, feeling the sensation of relaxation taking over [10 sec] ... Once more now, clench your left hand into a fist, notice the tension in the forearm ... and now ... let go. Letting your fingers spread out and relax ... noticing the difference between muscular tension and muscular relaxation. [10 sec] ...

Now repeat the same process with the right hand. Clench the right fist ... study the tension [5 sec] ... and now ... let go ... Notice the difference between tension and relaxation. Enjoy the contrast [10 sec] ... Once again now, clench the right fist ... focus on the tension and now ... let go. Relax the hand, letting the fingers spread out comfortably. Notice the difference between tension and relaxation. Notice the looseness beginning to develop in the left and right arms and hands. Enjoy this sense of relaxation.

Now bend both hands back at the wrists so that you are tensing the muscles in the back of the hand and in the forearm ... your fingers pointing towards the ceiling. Study the tension and now ... relax. Let your hands return to their resting positions and notice the difference between tension and relaxation. [10 sec] ... Once again bend both hands back, fingers pointing toward the ceiling, feeling the tension developing in the back of the hands and in the forearms, and now ... relax ... letting go further and further [10 sec] ...

Now clench both your hands into fists and bring them towards your shoulders so as to tighten your biceps, the large muscles in the upper part of the arm. Feel the tension in the biceps ... and now ... relax ... Letting your arms drop to your sides and notice the difference between tension and relaxation [10 sec] ... Doing that again now ... clench both hands, bringing both arms up to your shoulders, holding the tension in the biceps ... study the tension ... and now ... relax. Keep letting go of those muscles further and further [10 sec] ...

Now direct your attention to the shoulder area. Shrug your shoulders, bringing them up as if you were going to touch your ears. Notice the tension in your shoulders and in your neck. Study the tension ... hold it ... and now ... relax ... Letting both shoulders return to a resting position. Keep letting go further and further. Notice the contrast between tension and relaxation ... feel the relaxation spreading in your shoulder area [10 sec] ... Once again, bring both shoulders up as if you were going to touch your ears ... feel the tension in the shoulders, upper back and in the neck. Study the tension ... and now ... relax ... letting your shoulders come down to a resting position and noticing the contrast between tension and relaxation [10 sec] ...

And now you will begin to relax the various muscles of the face. Wrinkle up your forehead and brow, wrinkling it as much as you can ... feel the tension ... hold the tension ... and now ... relax ... feel the forehead smooth out ... all the muscles becoming loose. [10 sec]. Doing it once again ... wrinkle up the forehead ... hold the tension in the muscles above the eyes and in the forehead region ... and now ... relax ... noticing the contrast between tension and relaxation [10 sec] ...

Now close the eyes very tightly ... close them tightly so that you can feel the tension in the muscles around your eyes ... [5 sec] ... and now ... relax ... notice the difference between tension and relaxation ... [10 sec]. Once again, tightly close the eyes and study the tension ... hold it ... [5 sec] ... and now ... relax ... letting your eyes remain comfortably closed ... [10sec].

Now clench your jaws, bite your teeth together ... study the tension throughout the jaws ... [5 sec]... and now ... relax, letting your lips fall slightly open and noticing the difference between tension and relaxation in your jaw area ... [10 sec]. Once again ... clench the jaws ... study the tension ... [5 sec]... and now ... relax ... letting go further and further ... [10 sec].

Now purse your lips, pressing them tightly together ... feel the tension around the mouth ... and now ... relax ... relax all the muscles around the mouth letting your chin rest comfortably ... [10 sec]. Once again now, press your lips together ... study the tension, hold it ... and now ... relax ... Begin to notice how loose the various muscles that you have tensed and relaxed have become ... your hands, forearms, upper arms, shoulders and facial muscles.

Now bring your attention to your neck. Press your head back against the surface on which it is resting. Press it back so that you can feel the tension, primarily in the back of the neck and in the upper back. Hold it ... study it ... and now relax ... letting your head rest comfortably ... enjoying the contrast between tension and relaxation. Once again, press the head back ... feel the tension ... holding it and now ... relax ... letting go further and further ... [10 sec].

Now bring your head forward and try to bury your chin into your chest ... feel the tension ... hold it ... [5 sec] and now let go... relaxing further and further ... [10 sec]. Do this once again ... chin buried in the chest ... hold it ... [5 sec] ... and now ... relax ... relaxing further and further ... [10 sec].

Now bringing your attention to your back... arch your back , pushing out your chest and stomach so that you feel the tension in your back ... study the tension... hold it and now ... relax ... letting the body rest back where it was ... noticing the difference between tension and relaxation ... [10 sec]. Once again, arch the back way up ... study the tension... hold it ... [5 sec]... and now let go ... feeling all the muscles of the back becoming more and more relaxed ... [10 sec].

Now take a deep breath, filling up your lungs ... hold the breath ... study the tension throughout your chest and in your stomach area ... hold it ... and now ... relax...exhaling and continuing to breath as you were, noticing the difference between tension and relaxation ... [10 sec]. Doing that once more ... take a deep breath ... hold it ... study the tension... notice the muscles tensing ... and now ... relax ... exhaling and returning to normal breathing ... Feel the muscles of the chest and stomach becoming more and more relaxed each time you exhale ... [10 sec].

Now tighten the muscles in your stomach ... holding the tension ... making the stomach hard ... and now relax ... letting the muscles become loose ... [10 sed]. Doing that once again ... tighten the stomach muscles ... hold the tension and now ... relax ... relaxing further and further ... When you think you have relaxed as far as you can, relax further still ... [10 sec].

Now stretch both legs ... stretch them out so that you can feel the tension in the thighs ... stretch them way out ... [5 sec] and now relax ... Notice the difference between tension and relaxation... enjoy the sensation of relaxation ... [10 sec]. Once again, stretch out both legs... feeling the tension... the muscles becoming very hard ... and now ... relax ... all tension simply draining away ... [10 sec].

Now tense both calf muscles by pointing your toes towards your head... feel the muscles pulling ... feel the tightness in your calf and in your shins ... study the tension and now ... relax ... noticing the difference between tension and relaxation ... [10 sec]. Once again, bend both feet back at the ankles, feeling the tension ... hold it ... and now ... relax ... relaxing the muscles further and further ... more and more relaxed ... [10 sec].

Now, we will review all the muscle groups you have been working on. As I name each muscle group notice if there is any tension in those muscles ... if there is any tension send the message of relaxation to them and allow them to loosen and relax ... First relaxing the muscles in your feet, ankles and calves ... shins, knees and thighs ... buttocks and hips ... loosen all the muscles of your lower body ... relax your stomach, waist, lower back ... upper back, chest and shoulders ... relaxing your upper arms, forearms, and hands, right to the tips of your fingers ... Let the muscles of your throat and neck loosen ... Relax your jaw and facial muscles ... allowing all the muscles of your body to become loose ... Now remain in your position for a few minutes quietly with your eyes closed ... [2 mins].

OK now I am going to count from 1 to 5 ... when I reach the count of 5, open your eyes, feeling wide awake and fresh ... 5 ... 4 ... 3 ... 2 ... 1 ... eyes open and wide awake.

AUTOGENIC RELAXATION

To begin this exercise lie down or sit upright in a comfortable position. Loosen any tight clothing, uncross your legs and rest your arms by your sides or in you lap.

Close your eyes.

Become aware of your breathing ... breathing easily and naturally ... being aware of the natural rhythm of your breath as it flows in and out ... in and out ...

Feeling yourself becoming quieter and stiller ... quieter and stiller ...

Think to yourself 'relax' each time you breath out and feel the tension in your body draining away ...

1. Now become aware of your right arm ... first your right hand ...send the message of relaxation to your right hand each time you breath out ... feel your right hand becoming more and more relaxed as you let go of any tension in it ...

Now bring your attention to your right forearm ... relax your right forearm ... now relax your upper arm ...and now relax your right shoulder ... Feel your whole right arm becoming more and more relaxed ... becoming warm and heavy ...

2. Now bring your attention to your left hand ... send the message of relaxation to your left hand ... now relax your forearm ... now relax your upperarm ... and now your shoulder ... feel your whole left arm becoming warm and heavy ... more and more relaxed ...

3. Now bring your attention to your right leg ... first your right foot ... send the message of relaxation to your right foot ... feel the muscles in your foot soften as you let go of any tension there ... now relax your right calf ... now relax your thigh ... feel your whole right leg becoming warm and heavy ... your whole leg becoming more and more relaxed ...

4. Now bring your attention to your left foot ... send the message of relaxation to your left foot ... feel the muscles in your foot soften as you let go of any tension there ... now relax your calf ... now relax your thigh ... feel your whole left leg becoming warm and heavy ... your whole left leg becoming more and more relaxed ...

5. Now bring your attention to your torso ... first the stomach ... feel the muscles in your stomach becoming soft and loose ...soft and loose ... now bring your attention to your chest ... let go of any tightness in your chest ... feeling your chest becoming more and more relaxed ... your breathing becoming easier ... and easier ... Now become aware of your back ... send the message of relaxation to your back ... feel out any tight spots and let the tension simply dissolve ... your whole back feeling more and more relaxed ... Now bring your attention to your buttocks ... feel the muscles begin to soften ... letting go of any tension ... And now your whole front and back feeling warm and heavy ...

Now bring your attention to your neck ... send the message of relaxation to your neck ... feeling out any tight spots ... and allowing the tension to dissolve ... feel your neck becoming warm and soft ... more and more relaxed ...

Now bring your attention to your head ... first your face ... let the facial muscles relax and let go ... feel the lines smooth out ... allow the jaw to sag a little ... and the lips fall gently open ... relax the muscles around the eyes ... now relax your forehead ... feel your whole face becoming smooth and serene ...

Feel your whole body becoming warm and heavy ... your whole body becoming more and more relaxed ...

And now imagine a beautiful, tranquil scene ... any one that you enjoy ... and experience being in the scene ... take time to enjoy the tranquillity and peacefulness of the scene ... [1 min]

And now bring yourself out of the scene and become aware once again of your breathing ... think of your breath as a friend you always have inside you ... one who will always be there to calm you whenever you need it ...

Now when you are ready ... take time to bring yourself back to the room ... opening your eyes ... feeling fresh and alert ...

Further Reading

PRACTICAL BOOKS:

BURNS, David, *Feeling Good*, New American Library, New York, 1980 — An excellent account of how different thinking styles influence our lives.

DAVIS, Martha (Elizabeth Eshelman and Matthew McKay), *The Relaxation & Stress Reduction Workbook* [3rd Ed.], New Harbinger Publications, Oakland, 1988 — This is a bestselling large-format book that covers just about everything you would want to know about relaxation and well-being. It covers lots of practical activities you can use.

GREEN, Barry (with W. Timothy Gallwey), *The Inner Game of Music,* Pan Original, London, 1987 — This book adapts the ideas of Timothy Gallwey, who wrote *The Inner Game of Tennis*, to music. It contains some excellent exercises and very definitely promotes the mental side of performing.

ORLICK, Terry, *Psyching For Sport: Mental Training For Athletes*, Leisure Press, Champaign, Illinois, 1986 — Provides practical examples of how sports psychologists work with elite athletes to achieve peak performance.

TAYLOR, Jim (and C. Taylor), *Psychology of Dance*, Human Kinetics, Champaign, Illinois, 1995 — Provides practical examples of how sports psychology can be applied to dance.

INFORMATION BOOKS:

CSIKSZENTMIHALYI, Mihaly, *Flow: The Psychology Of Happiness*, Rider, London, 1992 — This is an inspiring account of research into the 'flow' experience and how people from all walks of life can experience it. It's more of an information book than a 'how to' book.

SALMON, Paul (and Robert Meyer), *Notes From The Green Room: Coping with Stress and Anxiety In Musical Performance*, Lexington Books, New York, 1992 — This provides a well researched account by two psychologists on how stress and anxiety affect performing.

STANTON, Rosemary, *Eating For Peak Performance*, Allen & Unwin, Sydney, 1988 — Provides information on diet and how this affects your level of physical performance.

Bibliography

BOURNE, Edmund, *The Anxiety and Phobia Workbook* [2nd Ed.], New Harbinger Publications, Oakland, 1995.

BUCHAN, Vivian, *Making Presentations With Confidence,* Barron's Educational Series, Hauppauge, New York, 1991.

BUCHANAN, Dominic, 'Bark Without Barf' in *Sydney Morning Herald*, 27 July 1994.

BYRNE, Robert, *1,911 Best Things Anybody Ever Said,* Fawcett Columbine, New York, 1988.

CSIKSZENTMIHALYI, Mihaly, *Flow: The Psychology of Happiness*, Rider, London, 1992.

COCHRANE, Peter, 'Michael is frank about stage fright' in *Sydney Morning Herald*, 5 May 1992.

FOWLES, Jib, *Starstruck: Celebrity Performers and the American Public*, Smithsonian Institution Press, Washington, 1992.

HALLETT, Bryce, 'West End Story' in *Weekend Australian*, 25–26 February 1995.

HAY, Peter, *Broadway Anecdotes*, Oxford University Press, New York, 1989.

HINES, Jerome, *Great Singers on Great Singing*, Limelight Editions, New York, 1994 (originally published, Doubleday, New York, 1982).

JACKSON, Sue, 'Athletes in Flow: A Qualitative Investigation of Flow States in Elite Figure Skaters' in *Journal of Applied Sport Psychology* 4 pp 161–80, 1992.

————, 'Factors Influencing the Occurence of Flow State in Elite Athletes' in *Journal of Applied Sport Psychology* 7 pp 138–166, 1995.

KIMBALL, Kathleen (Robin Petersen and Kathleen Johnson), *The Music Lover's Quotation Guide: A Lyrical Companion, Sound and Vision*, Toronto Canada, 1990.

KOHUT, Joe (John Kohut) [ed.], *Rock Talk: The Great Rock and Roll Quote Book*, Faber and Faber, Boston, 1994.

LUSETICH, Robert, 'Comedy's Grand Pianist' in *Weekend Australian*, 11–12 February 1995.

MARX, Groucho, *Groucho Marx and Other Short Stories and Tall Tales,* Penguin (extracted in *Sydney Morning Herald*, 17 April 1995).

NEWMAN, Barbara, *Striking a Balance: Dancers Talk About Dancing* [revised], Limelight Editions, New York, 1992 (originally published, Houghton Mifflin, Boston,

1982).

ROLAND, David, 'Stage Fright: If You're Not Nervous You're Dead' in *Rolling Stone*, Australia, July 1993.

SINDEN, Donald [ed.], *The Everyman Book of Theatrical Anecdotes*, J M Dent, London, 1987.

SPOTO, Donald, *Laurence Olivier: A Biography*, HarperPaperbacks, New York, 1993.

TALENT, Waits, 'Wings Joyce Morgan' in *Weekend Australian*, 20–21 August 1994.

THARP, Twyla, *Push Comes to Shove*, Bantam, New York, 1992.

WILLIAMS, Sue, 'Comedians Stand Up to be Counted' in *Australian* 20 April 1994.

YAMAN, Ebru, 'Grande Dame of the Ballet Stays on Her Toes' in *Weekend Australian*, 20–21 August 1994.

OTHER CURRENCY TITLES OF INTEREST

The Singing Voice by Pat Wilson

Landing a job on the strength of your voice is one of the most exciting things that can happen to any performer — whether singer, actor, dancer or musician — but it won't happen unless you maintain yourself and your voice in good shape and know the requirements of the industry.

This concise, intelligent, helpful, funny and eminently readable book will show you how to keep that voice of yours in good trim and how to tackle the tough world of auditions, rehearsals, long runs, tours, sound studios and much more.

All in Good Timing by Henri Szeps
Foreword by Leo McKern

Henri Szeps's passion for acting is infectious. Here Henri lays before the reader 30 years of acting experience and divulges his personal view on what good acting is all about. At the heart of good acting is good timing. Around this central theme Henri Szeps illustrates the mechanisms and devices needed to produce a convincing and truthful performance.

Masterclass: Women by Dean Carey
Masterclass: Men by Dean Carey

These two volumes contain close to 100 monologues by authors from around the world. They provide an arsenal of audition pieces for young actors — from classics such as Chekhov and Racine, to moderns including Berkoff, Gems, Henley, Miller, Thomson and Williamson.

In an extensive introductory section Dean Carey redefines and outlines the essential acting components and illuminates the creative process practically and passionately.

Auditioning for Musicals by Peter Mapleson

Written in a lively and confidence-inspiring style, this book contains practical advice for all actors, singers and dancers planning to audition for any musical production, with advice on preparation, technique, choice of material, rehearsing a song, readings and improvisation, and what to expect on the day.